divorceZen

escaping the divorce mindset

William Henry

Copyright © 2022 William Henry

First edition 2022

All rights reserved. No part of this book may be reproduced or transmitted in any form or by any means, electronic or mechanical, including photocopying, recording or any information storage or retrieval system without permission from the copyright holder.

The Author has made every effort to trace and acknowledge sources/resources/individuals. In the event that any images/information have been incorrectly attributed or credited, the Author will be pleased to rectify these omissions at the earliest opportunity.

ISBN 978-1-77636-274-5

Published by William Henry using Reach Publishers' services,
P O Box 1384, Wandsbeck, South Africa, 3631

Edited by Nikki Burnett for Reach Publishers
Website: www.reachpublishers.org
E-mail: reach@reachpublish.co.za

William Henry

For Y and C

Table of Contents

1.	Introduction	7
2.	A Thunderstorm Cannot Destroy the Sky – You Are Not Your Divorce	11
3.	You Are Not The Past; You Are Not The Future – You Are Now	15
4.	Taming the Wild Monkey Mind – You Are Not Your Thoughts and Emotions	24
5.	When Things Go Wrong, Don't Go With Them – You Are Not Your Reactions	33
6.	Don't Get Stung to Death by One Bee – You Don't Have to Bear a Grudge	43
7.	Go Out On a Limb! Peek Over the Edge! – You Don't Need Security	54
8.	What is Mindfulness?	68
9.	How to Practice Mindfulness	82

10.	The Pillars of Mindfulness – Surrender to Life	95
11.	The Pillars of Mindfulness – Non-Judgment and Non-Attachment	106
12.	Ego and Self-Awareness	119
13.	Wholeness (The Illusion of Separateness)	131
14.	Non-Doing (Being) and Stillness (Space)	138
15.	Fear and Anxiety	145
16.	Victimhood and Anger	152
17.	Unhappiness	160
18.	Patience	167
19.	Forgiveness	174
20.	The Journey Ahead	182

1

Introduction

When I started on this journey, I was a divorce lawyer. I felt compelled by the profound suffering I saw every day to write this book.

I came to realize that shepherding my clients through the legal process alone was not enough. I felt like I was only 'hacking at the leaves' of the problem, as Stephen Covey put it. I was not 'cutting at the root' of divorce; I was not helping my clients to overcome the paralyzing and defeating thoughts and the destructive patterns of behavior that were the true source of their suffering.

A client once said to me: 'Yesterday was the worst day of my life, and tomorrow, I'm sure, I will say the same about today. I am sad, hurt, and lonely. As time presses forward, all I can do is to press forward too if I don't want to get trampled by life.'

There's no way around it, divorce is 'the dark night of the soul'. It overwhelms us and leaves us feeling disappointed, angry, lonely, fearful, helpless, hopeless, and defeated. We question everyone we've ever trusted and everything we've ever held dear. Separating from our partners rocks the very foundation of our being.

The bad news is that the pain is inevitable. The good news is that the suffering is optional.

Your current life situation – divorce – causes the pain. You cannot change the reality of divorce because you don't control it. Even if you move the proverbial mountain to try to save your marriage, if your partner is unwilling there is nothing you can do. You cannot clap with one hand. It is as it is. And it is painful.

But the suffering is caused by your mind. And because it is *your* mind, *you do* control it. *You can* stop the suffering. But how?

To lose the suffering, you have to lose your mind. I don't mean that you have to lose your sanity. You just have to lose your 'wild monkey mind', as a wise person put it. You have to get rid of the endless stream of thoughts about your divorce which, like wild monkeys, 'incessantly swing from branch to branch' inside your head.

Introduction

This book has been ten years in the making. About a year into writing it, my own marriage fell apart and, suddenly, my clients' suffering became deeply personal. I was forced to start taking the medicine that I'd been doling out to others for years.

For a long time, I couldn't write anything. I just practiced living the principles in this book. The journey has been worth it. When I finally started writing again, I could draw, not only on the collective experiences of my clients, but also on my own painful experiences and what I had learned to help me overcome them.

Let me start by clearly stating what this book is not. Despite the title, this is not a Buddhist guide to divorce. I just like the word 'zen', because in my mind it conjures up images of peace and serenity, like a tree by a stream on a clear summer's day.

This book is short by design. Your anxious mind already has enough information to absorb on a daily basis and I don't want to pile on more. Besides, my message is simple. I don't need hundreds of pages to explain it.

All I want to do is to help you take control of your thoughts, so that you can then let go of the toxic and unhelpful ones. I want to show you a mindset that can guide you through one of the most traumatic life events, without any more needless suffering.

Einstein said that we cannot solve our problems at the same level of thinking that we were at when we created those problems in the first place. Escaping the misery of divorce requires a radical shift in mindset.

Let's begin.

2

A Thunderstorm Cannot Destroy the Sky – You Are Not Your Divorce

> Never let a cloudy day ruin your sunshine,
> for even if you can't see it,
> the sunshine is still there, inside of you,
> ready to shine when you will let it.
>
> - Amy Pitzele

A client once described her experience to me in the following way: 'Going through a divorce is like falling overboard and being swept away by a raging river – you suddenly find yourself in an all-consuming fight for survival against currents and rapids and rocks and debris.'

It is this mindset that was at the heart of my client's suffering.

Going through a divorce is nothing like falling into a river. If you fall into a river, it's possible that you might drown or get smashed against the rocks. Falling into a river might cost you your very *life*. Divorce only affects your *life situation*.

Can you see that it's a question of perspective?

If your mindset is that divorce threatens your very life – instead of only affecting your life situation – you lose all perspective. If you experience divorce as falling into a river and being swept away by the current, it will demand all of your attention and focus, and it will consume all of your energy and effort to simply 'keep your head above water'.

But if you only experience divorce as a dangerous river that you have to cross – something unpleasant that you have to deal with, but also something that is separate from who you are (your identity) – then you can objectively assess the dangers from the safety of the riverbank, and you can calmly reflect on how best to navigate a crossing.

I don't mean to minimize the impact of divorce on your life. Divorce is undoubtedly one of the most traumatic life events that can happen to anyone. It's a tornado that touches down, often without warning, and roars through your life, destroying a partnership that you thought would endure forever, tearing apart your children's sense of security, and leaving a financial wasteland in its wake.

But divorce cannot destroy *you*. Think of your life – the life that you are – as a deep lake (we'll return to this image throughout). Life situations happen on the surface of the lake. The surface is sometimes calm, sometimes choppy, and sometimes – as with the life situation of divorce – a squall blasts across the water and violent swells capsize boats.

But no matter what happens on the surface, deep down the lake is always the same – calm and still.

Know that whatever you experience on the surface of your life is ultimately not who you are. You cannot build your identity on life situations that are transient, that come and go randomly. When you know yourself as the lake deep down – the true you – whatever happens on the surface of your life will no longer be a life and death struggle.

The intense suffering you experience in divorce creates the illusion that you're isolated. As Eckhart Tolle puts it: 'You're like a ray of sunlight that has forgotten that it's an inseparable part of the sun.' You're miserable because you think that you're alone with your fear, anger, sadness, and disappointment, and that you have to fight for your very survival.

Realize deeply that *you* are infinitely greater than the life situation of divorce. Just as there is room in the sky for a thunderstorm, there is room in *the life that you are* for divorce. And, just as a storm doesn't have the power to destroy the sky, so the life situation of divorce doesn't have the power to destroy *you*.

Many people in the throes of divorce are so consumed by their particular 'divorce drama' that they can't wait to share it with anyone who would listen. It's all they talk about. 'Divorce' becomes their identity.

Don't turn divorce into your identity. Don't let it torment your every waking moment and haunt your dreams. Don't let it become all that you think about and talk about. Don't give divorce a power over you that it doesn't have on its own.

Don't allow yourself to become so overwhelmed by the *life situation* of divorce that you lose your sense of *life*.

Recognize divorce for what it is: a painful and disruptive – but also *temporary* – life situation.

Divorce is not your life. It's not who you are.

> Let us remember that within us
> there is a palace of immense magnificence.
>
> - Teresa of Avilla

3

You Are Not The Past; You Are Not The Future – You Are Now

> The past cannot be regained, although we can learn from it;
> the future is not yet ours, even though we must plan for it…
> we have only today.
>
> - Charles Hummell

Once, when I advised a client to see a psychotherapist to help her deal with the trauma of divorce, she said to me: 'I don't need to see a shrink. I know exactly what I feel. These days I only ever experience three feelings: sadness, anger, and fear. I'm profoundly sad for the children when I remember those wonderful summers we spent as a family at the lake; we were so close. Then, I am furious with Kevin for his betrayal and the break-up of our family. And then I become deeply fearful about the future. What will happen to me financially? What will the long-term effect of the divorce be on the kids? Then the sadness starts all over again.'

Many of us have mastered the neurotic art of spending much of our lives allowing past problems and future concerns to dominate the present moment. We end up feeling anxious, frustrated, depressed, and hopeless.

When you start paying attention to where your mind is, from moment to moment throughout the day, you'll find that you spend a considerable amount of time clinging to memories, being absorbed in reverie, and regretting things that have already happened and are over. You'll also find that you spend at least as much energy anticipating, planning, worrying, and fantasizing about the future.

The present moment – *now* – is the only time you have, and it's the only time over which you have any control.

> I can feel guilty about the past,
> apprehensive about the future,
> but only in the present can I act.
>
> - Abraham Maslow

Now is the Only Time You Ever Have

One of the major causes of suffering in divorce is your constant reliving of the dead past and fearful obsessing about the imagined future. Your attachment to the past and the future causes suffering, because neither the past nor the future is real. The past ('memory') and the future ('anticipation') exist only as creations of your imagination.

The problem is that you can't cope with things that aren't real, things that are only concepts constructed by your mind. You can only cope with something that's real. Only the present moment is real.

> We have only this moment,
> sparkling like a star in our hand...
> and melting like a snowflake.
> Let us use it before it is too late.
>
> - Marie Benyon Ray

Think about it: There is never a time when your life is not *this moment*. Life happens *now*. Past or future moments only exist when you remember or anticipate them. Nothing has ever happened in the past. It happened in the now. Nothing will ever happen in the future. It will happen in the now. *Right now* is all you have to work with.

> He who lives in the present, lives in eternity.
>
> - Ludwig Wittgenstein

You can get rid of a major source of suffering in your life by realizing deeply that the present moment is all you ever have. All you ever have to deal with in real life – as opposed to the imaginary mind creations of past and future – is *this moment*.

The answer that you've been seeking, the strength to face your partner across a lawyer's conference room table, the kindness of a neighbour pitching in to look after your children because you have to be in court and the babysitter cancelled, will be there in the moment when you need it – not before, not after.

Consciously choose to give up your attachment to past and future and make the present moment the primary focus of your life.

You might ask: 'What's so great about the present moment? My present moment is filled with the trauma of divorce. I don't want to be in the present moment. I'd rather be reliving the past or daydreaming about some happier future.'

The present moment is the only time that you have in which to live, to grow, to feel, to heal, to act, to learn, and to change.

There are three ways, in which you might dishonor the present moment when going through divorce. You can treat the present moment as:

1. a steppingstone to a better future
2. a problem to overcome
3. an enemy to resist

In dealing with the life situation of divorce, perhaps you see the present moment only as a *steppingstone* to a moment in the future that you believe will be more important than this moment. This is often the case, even when you know intellectually that any future moment is only a figment of your imagination, and that it will only manifest itself as the present moment. The fundamental problem is that you're never fully present, because you are always striving to get to a better future moment.

The same mental dynamics that convince you that 'someday' will be better, will only repeat themselves so that 'someday' never actually comes. The result is that you miss out on life.

Perhaps you're impatient, frustrated, and stressed out all the time because you believe that the life situation of divorce is a *problem to solve.* And until you've solved 'this problem', you can never be happy, fulfilled, or start a new life – or so you believe.

But, as you know from experience, as soon as you solve one problem, another one rears its ugly head. Before you know it, you live in a world entirely made up of problems and your life becomes an endless game of whack-a-mole. As long as you perceive the present moment as a problem, there can be no end to your problems.

Perhaps you treat the present moment as an *enemy to resist.* You actively fight against it. You complain about how slow and inefficient the court system is. You curse your partner for leaving the family or for forcing you to leave. You blame your lawyer, or the mediator, or the judge.

When the voice in your head is constantly complaining, accusing, and blaming, you struggle against *what is*, against what is always already the case – the present moment. Resisting the present moment is a useless waste of energy because it accomplishes nothing.

The crucial question to ask yourself, as often as you can, is:

> How do I see the present moment?

The only way to go beyond an agonizing relationship with the present moment, is to become *aware.* You have to pause long enough to let the present moment sink in, long enough to hold the present moment in awareness – to feel it and to experience its fullness.

Anxiety, stress, and frustration flood your mind the moment you turn your back on the present moment. You turn your back on the present moment when you believe that something else – a sad memory or a worrisome thought about the future – is more important.

Do you see how one small misunderstanding, one small flaw in your thought process, creates so much suffering?

To purge your life from suffering, live by, and repeat to yourself as often as you remember, this motto:

Be. Here. Now!

As we'll see in later chapters, the whole point of the practice of mindfulness is to drag your attention (sometimes kicking and screaming) away from your never-ending brooding over the past or worrying about the future, into the present moment.

No other moment in the past or in the future can ever be more important than the present moment.

The Present Moment Shapes Your Future

You might think that your deliverance from the hell of divorce lies at some point in the future. But what you don't realize is that whatever future outcome you desire, it is inextricably woven together with all the actions that lead up to it. What you do in the present moment determines what you will experience in any future moment.

It's in the present moment that you create the future, because the present moment is the only place where you can make positive changes in your life that will shape your future. If the steps you're taking now are filled with anger, stress, worry, and negativity, so, too, will your desired future moment be filled with all that unhappiness. You will only re-create modified versions of the same world again and again.

The step you're taking right now embodies all your future moments, all your desired outcomes, everything you want your life to be after divorce. But, ultimately, there is always only the one step you're taking right now. So, give the present moment your fullest attention.

To focus on the step that you're taking right now doesn't mean that you don't have a destination in mind, or that you don't have a plan (planning might well be the only thing you can do in the present moment). It simply means that the destination is far less important than the step you're taking right now. That's because the quality of the destination – that future moment of salvation that you long for – will depend entirely on the quality of the step that you're taking at this moment.

> It is good to have an end
> to journey toward,
> but it is the journey
> that matters in the end.
>
> - Ursula le Guin

The best way, then, to prepare for any future moment is to be fully aware in the present. Your *intention* may be for a better future, but your *attention* is in the present.

> Light tomorrow with today.
>
> - Elizabeth Barret Browning

After all, it's not that 'today is the first day of the rest of your life', as the saying goes. It's that today – the present moment – is all there is to your life. You have only now. Embrace it.

> This is the day which the Lord has made.
> Let us rejoice and be glad in it.
>
> - Psalm 118:24

4

Taming the Wild Monkey Mind – You Are Not Your Thoughts and Emotions

> The mind is its own place,
> and in itself,
> can make heaven of Hell,
> and hell of Heaven.
>
> - John Milton

In divorce, your worst enemy is not your partner. Your worst enemy lurks between your ears. It is the voice in your head.

Thoughts

Almost every one of us suffers from what Eckhart Tolle calls *'the disease of compulsive thinking'*. We so identify with the constant stream of negative and destructive thoughts, which our minds crank out in an endless, repetitive loop, that we've lost the ability to stop thinking.

I can hear you asking incredulously: 'Why would I ever want to stop thinking? The ability to think differentiates us from all other species. The mind is mysterious and miraculous beyond compare.'

The mind is indeed a remarkable tool – if used correctly. The problem is that most of us don't use our minds. *Our minds use us.* In fact, we don't really think. Thinking happens to us.

As a wise person once said: 'My thinking mind is a perfect servant and a lousy master.' Our minds take us over completely. We don't even realize that the mind has become the master, and we its slave.

If you don't believe me, try this: Stop thinking for a moment. Not so easy, is it? The mind runs after anything and everything – a memory, a sense impression, a sight, or a sound can capture your thinking mind and pull it away. As a consequence, at that moment and for however long your attention is captured, you're quite literally 'lost' in your thoughts. You live immersed in a seemingly uncontrollable, never-ending stream of thoughts, coming willy-nilly, one after the other in rapid succession.

Especially for people going through divorce, compulsive thinking can become an addiction. The compulsion arises because you live almost exclusively through memory (the past) and anticipation (the future) as you try to escape the dreadful life situation of divorce (the present).

Most of us are burdened with what Buddhists call the *'monkey mind'*, the thoughts that 'swing from limb to limb, stopping only to scratch themselves, spit, and howl'. As Elizabeth Gilbert puts it: 'From the distant past to the unknowable future, my mind swings wildly through time, touching on dozens of ideas per minute, unharnessed and undisciplined.' We don't feel as if we have much choice about where the monkey will leap next.

Your mind has tremendous momentum. It can drag you along like a wild horse to places you probably don't want to go, and to which you might not even realize you're heading.

Why are our monkey minds a problem? Because the more we identify with our minds, with the voice in our heads that we hear non-stop, the more we suffer.

The voice – the noisy, soul devouring chatter that relentlessly rattles around in your head – truly becomes your own worst enemy. Countless times every day it pounces, beats you up, and robs you of the energy, creativity, and motivation that are so essential to sustain you through the divorce process.

When going through my own divorce, it took me some time to realize two facts which, in hindsight, seem remarkably obvious.

First, all of the time and energy that I had been pouring into my resentful internal diatribe served no purpose whatsoever. The voice was just ricocheting around my own head, turning it into a foolish echo chamber. It had no effect on my partner at all.

Second, the voice did not bring me any relief. When I started blaming my partner, the noisy chatter in my mind just got louder and louder, leaving me more agitated and miserable.

You probably also think the same negative and destructive thoughts over and over again in endless, repetitive cycles. And then the fear, anxiety, regret, guilt, anger, and sadness threaten to overwhelm you.

The voice constantly comments, judges, and complains. And the commenting, judging, and complaining most often don't have anything to do with the situation in which you find yourself at that moment. The voice in your head is usually either delving into the past and rehashing unpleasant memories or stirring up images of things going wrong in the future.

But seldom does the voice rest in the *present moment*. It is only in the present moment that we can experience the depthless and abiding peace that passes all understanding – the peace of God. That's because God is right here, right now, and the present moment is the only place to find Him.

Emotions

As if compulsive thinking in itself is not enough of a destructive force in your life, there are of course also the emotions that attach themselves to your incessant, negative, and fearful thoughts. Simply put, an emotion is the body's reaction to a thought. The voice in the head tells a story that the body believes in and reacts to. The more you identify with your mind, the stronger the emotional charge in your body becomes.

In divorce, which for most people is a time of crisis and emotional upheaval, your thoughts predominantly carry a highly negative and pessimistic emotional charge. There's the suffering of self-condemnation when you blame yourself for something you did or didn't do. If you've hurt people, you might also experience the emotional pain of guilt. Of course, there's also a negative emotional charge in anger, anxiety, insecurity, worry, fear, loss, grief, embarrassment, despair, and hopelessness.

The problem is that the body, for all its wonderous design and abilities, cannot distinguish between a thought and reality. When you think about an argument that happened a month ago with your partner, your body experiences that memory as if you and your partner are screaming at each other face to face in that very moment.

Just thinking about the argument prompts the anger to boil up inside you, which in turn causes your heart to beat faster, your face to feel flushed, and your breath to quicken. But the emotion – the anger – has no outlet because the situation that caused it only exists in your mind as a memory. This pent-up emotional energy then generates more angry thoughts, and so the cycle of suffering continues.

How do we break this vicious cycle? How do we switch off our mental motors?

Taming the 'Wild Monkey Mind'

The sad truth is that our emotions are slaves to our thoughts, and we are slaves to our emotions.

However, the beginning of freedom is simply to become *aware* of your compulsive and incessant thinking. As we'll see, self-awareness is a uniquely human endowment; no plant or animal possesses it. Self-awareness allows us to 'stand apart from ourselves', in a sense, and to examine our own thoughts. In other words, it enables us to think about our very thought processes.

Awareness doesn't involve trying to change our thinking by thinking some more. Awareness lies beyond thought and is more like a vessel that contains our thinking. Awareness helps us to see and know our thoughts as thoughts, rather than getting caught up in them as reality.

The moment we start 'watching the thinker', as Eckhart Tolle puts it, we realize that we are not the 'thinker'; we are not our thoughts and emotions. We are the 'knower', the awareness behind our thoughts and emotions.

When you – as the knower – start watching the thinker, the total identification with the voice in your head dissolves. You realize: *There is the voice, and here I am being aware of it.* The moment you stop identifying with the voice, your thoughts – which generally are narrow, inaccurate, self-involved, and habitual to the point of being imprisoning – lose their power over you. You feel stillness and peace arising inside of you.

It's liberating to realize that you have the ability to focus your awareness where you wish, despite your mind's tendency to being grabbed, pushed, and pulled any which way by each thought.

Initially, it's difficult to sustain awareness for more than a few seconds. Before you know it, the wild horse of your compulsive thinking viciously drags you along again.

The key is to create a break in your mind stream every day as often as you can. That's what the practice of *mindfulness* is all about. It teaches you how to quiet your mind, how to use its energy to guide you rather than to tyrannize you.

Every day, as often as you can, ask yourself:

What is going on inside my mind right now?

If your mental motor is churning out a steady stream of useless, repetitive, and destructive thoughts – unpleasant memories or fearful future scenarios – create a break in your mind stream. Direct all of your attention and focus into the present moment. Remember, all that you ever have to deal with in reality – as opposed to imaginary mind projections – is *this moment.*

If you find this hard to do, start by focusing on your *breathing* (a technique that we'll examine in detail later). Being aware of your breathing forces you into the present moment by taking attention away from thinking. In this way you create inner space.

Take three conscious deep breaths.
Focus on the breath as it enters and leaves your body.

Three conscious breaths, taken many times a day, is an easy and effective way to bring space into your life and so to break the endless mind stream. Without these breaks in the mind stream, your thinking becomes repetitive, uninspired, and devoid of any creative spark.

It's in the space between thoughts that you realize that you are not your thoughts and feelings, that you don't have to believe in them, and that you certainly don't have to react to them or act on them.

Come to see your thoughts and emotions for what they are – just thoughts and emotions! They can't hurt you without your consent. There's nothing to hold your negative emotions in place except your own thoughts.

This is the only way to free yourself from a lifetime of being tyrannized by your mind.

> Such are your habitual thoughts,
> such also will be the character of your mind,
> for the soul is dyed
> by the colour of the thoughts.
>
> - Marcus Aurelius

5

When Things Go Wrong, Don't Go With Them – You Are Not Your Reactions

> A life of reaction is a life of slavery, intellectually and spiritually.
> One must fight for a life of action, not reaction.
>
> - Rita Mae Brown

Reactions (Conditioned Behaviors)

Most of us react like bundles of conditioned reflexes that are constantly being triggered by people and situations into predictable outcomes of behavior. We react just like the dogs in Pavlov's famous experiment. Someone says something to you that is rude or hurtful, and you react unconsciously in a predictable way – you attack, or you defend yourself, or you withdraw.

It's especially true during divorce that the interactions between you and your partner are governed by conditioned behaviors and reactions. Your partner knows just how to 'push your buttons'. You've come to believe that your reactions are simply automatically triggered by your partner.

As long as you live in your mind and allow your mind, with its conditioned blueprint of behavior, to run your life, you have no choice. You bear the heavy burden of anguish and conflict and despair. You are trapped in your own hell. Yours is a reality completely perverted by mistrust, fear, contempt, and resentment. You create suffering for yourself and others.

Through your reactivity, you tend to blow matters of little consequence out of all proportion. You overreact. A comment or a gesture by your partner that someone else would shrug off with a knowing smile or not even pay any attention to, becomes a source of intense suffering for you.

When you encounter problems or setbacks on the road of divorce, instead of being self-aware in the present moment, you react against the situation. You waste tremendous amounts of energy on fruitless complaining or aggravation – energy that could be used to solve the problem.

You might say of something that happens in your divorce: 'That's terrible.' But, the judge's decision, your partner's outburst, the children's antagonism – it's not terrible. *It is as it is.*

Life events have no inherent meaning. *You* are the narrator of your life. It's your reaction, and the emotion that your reaction creates, that are terrible.

> We are not troubled by things,
> but by our thoughts about things.
>
> - Epictetus

If you're in prison, for example, you have a choice: Resistance or surrender, enslavement to or liberation from external circumstances, misery and torment or deep, abiding peace.

> Two men look out through the same bars;
> one sees the mud and one the stars.
>
> - Frederick Langbridge

Two people go through difficult divorces. One uses divorce as an opportunity to strengthen his/her inner resources, while the other uses it as an excuse to abuse alcohol or drugs.

Each reaction to something that happens to you either adds to the quality of your life or takes away from it. Each so-called 'terrible' thing that happens in your divorce either opens your eyes to an opportunity to make a choice for the better or sends you into a bottomless pit of self-pity and suffering.

> A man is as miserable as he thinks he is.
>
> - Seneca

Between Stimulus and Response Lies the Freedom to Choose

The Austrian psychiatrist, Viktor Frankl, was trained in the Freudian paradigm of determinism. He believed that your experiences as a child shaped your character and personality and so governed the rest of your life. The limits of your life were set in early childhood and there was precious little you could do about it.

Frankl, together with his parents and his wife, were enslaved in the Nazi concentration camps. Frankl's wife and parents perished. Frankl was rotated through four of the camps during the war. He experienced torture, slave labor, starvation, and degradation so repugnant as to be almost beyond comprehension. Frankl quite literally stared death in the face every single day. His Nazi captors took everything from him – or so they thought.

One day, lying in his cell naked, starving, freezing, and filthy, Frankl became aware of what he later called *'the last of the human freedoms'*, the one freedom that the Nazis could never take away. This was:

> The freedom to choose one's attitude
> in any given set of circumstances,
> to choose one's own way.

The Nazis controlled every aspect of his environment, and they held the power of life and death over his body. But Frankl was still a self-aware being. He alone had the freedom to choose how his life circumstances were going to affect him.

In the midst of hell on earth, Viktor Frankl used *self-awareness* to discover a fundamental truth about human nature:

> Between stimulus and response,
> I have the freedom to choose.
> I have independent will.

You have the ability to act based on self-awareness, free from all other influences – your partner, your lawyer, the judge, or your financial circumstances.

There are so many things that happen to you in divorce that you can't change. But *you can change* the way your mind experiences and reacts to these events. Your sadness or anger doesn't have an independent existence outside of you. These emotions come from within. You have the power to conquer your emotions rather than letting them rule over you.

You may not have a choice about the things that happen to you, but *you can choose* the attitude you bring to anything that happens to you; *you can choose* your response. This is one of the greatest gifts that you can give yourself in divorce.

You and your partner tell yourselves absolute and inflexible stories of what kind of person the other is: 'She's just an angry person'; 'He always does this'. These stories you spin about each other have such potency and become so dominant that they can determine your reality. After all, if you perceive something as real, it can have real consequences.

Only through self-awareness – not through thinking – can you see the totality of your partner. Only through self-awareness are you able to see: *There is my partner and here is the anger I feel towards my partner.* Then you realize that there are other ways of dealing with your partner, instead of your conditioned, destructive reactions.

The external circumstances of your life didn't change at all. Your partner still does the exact same thing that used to drive you up the wall. The only thing that has changed is your mind. You don't take your partner's words and actions personally anymore.

> Every time you start to think that
> the problem is 'out there',
> stop yourself.
> That very thought is the problem.

You empower what's out there to control you. In other words, what's out there has to change before you can change. But change never happens from the outside in. You have to change from the inside out. Most often, it's your reaction to what happens to you that hurts you far more than what happens to you.

Be *'Response-able'*

If you are reactive, you are, quite literally, 'being lived'. You reactively live out the scripts prepared for your life by your parents, your partner, your children, society, and the pressures of circumstances.

Reactive people build their emotional lives around the behavior of other people, empowering the weakness of other people to control them.

In truth, you don't react to your partner or a situation that your partner creates. You react to your feelings towards your partner or the situation. They are *your* feelings, and your feelings are not someone else's fault.

You realize that *having* your feelings doesn't mean that you *are* your feelings. When you realize this truth fully, you can take responsibility for how you feel and consciously choose to change how you feel.

Your reaction is not automatically triggered by your partner. Your reaction is still a choice, although you make the choice unconsciously. If you become *self-aware* – by stepping back from your mind and witnessing these choices as you make them, you take the whole process from your unconscious mind to your conscious awareness.

You realize that if your partner insults you, instead of automatically being offended (unconscious reaction), *you can choose* not to be offended; *you can choose* to let the insult just 'pass through you' (conscious awareness). Shifting your perspective allows you choose from a place of awareness, where you're empowered rather than disempowered. Your partner no longer has the power to control your inner state. You are now in *your* power, not your partner's.

> No one can hurt you without your consent.
>
> - Eleanor Roosevelt

Your behavior is the product of your own conscious decisions, not your conditions. It's vital that you recognize this and take responsibility for the fact that you do have a choice in the way in which you respond to your partner and to the circumstances of your divorce.

Don't blame your partner, your past conditioning, or your circumstances for your behavior. Be responsible – *response-able* – for your life. 'Response-ability' means the ability to choose a creative response to your partner or the circumstance, rather than being carried away by reaction.

Do you see the difference between reaction, which is unconscious, and response, which is consciously chosen?

Don't Let Yesterday Hold Today Hostage

One of the great dangers of being trapped in reactivity is that it becomes a self-fulfilling prophesy. You become entrenched in the mindset that people and circumstances control your peace and happiness. You then look for evidence to support this fallacy. In other words, yesterday holds today hostage.

Some misfortunes you bring upon yourself; others are completely beyond your control. But no matter what happens to you, *you always have the power to choose* your interpretation of your life's events.

When you see things differently, you start thinking differently, feeling differently, and behaving differently. If you can change your mind, you can change your world.

As we've seen, the quality of your future is determined by the choices that you make in every moment. The more you are consciously aware of the choices you make, the more you will make choices that bring peace and happiness to you and to those around you.

When you're grounded in self-awareness, you're more likely to be creative and to see new options and new solutions to your problems. You're more likely to be aware of your thoughts and emotions and less likely to be carried away by them.

Out of all the choices available to you, there is one that will lead to peace for you and your loved ones. This choice leads to a form of behavior which Deepak Chopra calls *'spontaneous right action'*. This is the right action, at the right time, in response to something that your partner said or did. Spontaneous right action is the opposite of reaction. It is the right response to every situation as it happens.

6

Don't Get Stung to Death by One Bee – You Don't Have to Bear a Grudge

> In hatred, as in love,
> we grow like the thing we brood upon.
> What we loathe,
> we graft onto our very soul.
>
> - Mary Renault

Are you consumed by an obsessive hatred of your partner? Many people in the thick of divorce, and many more who have been divorced for years, carry a heavy burden of resentment. They feel bitter, angry, taken advantage of, insulted, or deeply wounded by things that their partners said and did. They live in a permanent state of 'me against my partner'.

Why do we bear grudges against our partners? More importantly, what good does it do for us to carry a grievance around with us, sometimes for many years?

Don't Keep Grudges (the Past) Alive

> To be wronged is nothing unless you continue to remember it.
>
> - Confucius

A grudge is a strong, negative emotion caused by your partner's words or actions in the past. You keep grudges alive by relentlessly thinking about them. You feed your grudges by telling the story over and over again to yourself and to others of 'what my partner did to me' or 'how my partner ruined my life'.

The problem with grudges is that they poison large parts of our lives. While we think about and feel our grudges (the past), their overpowering negative emotional charge might completely distort the way in which we experience something in the present. Grudges can incite us to do or say something to a loved one in the present moment that to an objective observer seems unprovoked or a total overreaction.

It's the malevolent influence of grudges that, at Christmas dinner, rouses you into making gratuitously nasty jabs at your partner or saying something about your partner that's just plain mean and that makes the children cringe.

> You will not advance even one inch
> closer to divinity
> as long as you cling to even one last
> seductive thread of blame.
> As smoking is to the lungs, so is
> resentment to the soul…
>
> - Elizabeth Gilbert

Every day that we bear a grudge is as if we ingest a bit of poison and expect the other person to die.

> Something of vengeance I had tasted for the
> first time;
> as aromatic wine it seemed,
> on swallowing, warm and racy;
> but it's after-flavour, metallic and corrosive
> as if I had been poisoned.
>
> - Charlotte Brontë

The suffering of divorce drives you deeper into your negative internal dialogue and causes your toxic emotions – all the anger, resentment, guilt, and shame – to fester inside you, screaming for your attention.

By complaining about your partner, judging him/her, criticizing everything he/she does or says, you strengthen your own false sense of who you are. In a negative sense, you remain married – you and your partner each needs the weakness of the other to justify your own ego's need for superiority.

But, when you're constantly judging and criticizing, it creates a lot of turbulence in your internal dialogue. You don't get ulcers from what you eat, but from what's eating you. So, what are all these grudges getting you (apart from ulcers)? Do they bring you comfort, joy, peace? Of course not.

> To carry a grudge is like being stung to death by one bee.
>
> - William H. Walton

I have seen people going through long and bitter divorce litigation, whose faces literally change in the process. Once beautiful, dignified faces become contorted into permanent scowls. Grudges make us suffer. We carry such a heavy burden of hate and anger and resentment that many times it feels as if we're going to be crushed under its weight.

> Hate smoulders and eventually destroys not the hated, but the hater.
>
> - Dorothy Thompson

This begs the question: 'Why do you want to hold on to the suffering? Why do you want to walk around for another day, another week, another month – or a lifetime – with the grudges of the past etched on your face?'

Consciously Choose Your Response

As we've seen, especially in intimate relationships, we react like bundles of conditioned reflexes that are triggered by our partners into predictable patterns of behavior. When your partner accuses you of something or doesn't acknowledge an act of kindness on your part, or invades your privacy, or starts arguing with you about something, the fear, anger, bitterness, and resistance well up inside of you and your mind scrambles to justify, to blame, or to retaliate. You react – you hurl an insult right back, you defend your position, or you withdraw and sulk.

The truth is, however, that feeling offended or hurt is a *choice*. It's not a choice that we make consciously, but it's still a choice. As Stephen Covey reminds us: 'It's our willing permission, our consent to what happens to us, that hurts us far more than what happens to us in the first place.'

As we've seen, when your partner insults you, instead of unconsciously falling back on your past conditioned behavior of being offended or hurt, you could make a different choice if you wanted to.

You could *choose* not to be offended or hurt. You could *choose* not to react at all. You could *choose* to be kind even if your partner is being a jerk.

When two people decide to be kind to each other, especially if they have children together and will have contact for many years to come, perhaps for the rest of their lives, they can find their way through their feelings of distrust, anger, and resentment, and give their children a gift of inestimable worth.

> Kindness is a hard thing to give away;
> it keeps coming back to the giver.
>
> - Ralph Scott

Every time that you feel the anger and bitterness well up inside of you, invite your partner silently in the words of the Sufi poet, Rumi:

> Out beyond ideas of wrongdoing and
> right doing there is a field.
> I will meet you there.

Consciously choosing your response is not denial. You don't pretend that negative thoughts and emotions don't arise. You admit that they're there. You examine them to gain insight into where they came from. You understand deeply that they don't have to control you. And then, with courage and compassion, you *choose* to let them go.

Make no mistake about it, it's a sacrifice to let go of familiar and comforting old grudges. A failed intimate relationship leaves us with a big heap of foul emotional garbage – anger, sadness, doubt, distrust, fear, loneliness.

Letting go of old grudges and negative thoughts and emotions takes practice and discipline. It's not a message we can hear once and expect to master instantly. It requires us to be ever watchful.

Just 'Flap Your Wings' And Carry On

All you need to break your grudges' chokehold on your life, to stop the drama and the insanity, is *self-awareness*. Only present moment awareness can relieve you of the heavy burden of the past that you carry with you. This requires that you become aware of the thoughts that keep the grudge alive, and that you feel the emotion that is the body's response to those thoughts.

Eckhart Tolle tells the story of two ducks in a pond. They peacefully float along, at ease with themselves, totally present. Sometimes one duck strays into the other duck's territory and they get into a fight. The fight usually lasts for only a few seconds, then the ducks separate, swim off in opposite directions, and vigorously flap their wings a few times. Thereafter, they continue to swim on peacefully as if the fight had never even happened.

Tolle says that watching the ducks made him realize that by flapping their wings they released surplus energy, thus preventing it from becoming trapped in their bodies and turning into negativity.

Of course, that's not what we humans do. When we get into a fight with our partners, we keep the fight alive by constantly thinking about it: *How dare you say that to me? You just sit around thinking up new ways to push my buttons. But I'll show you. Nobody says that to me and gets away with it!* And on and on we wax for days, weeks, or even years after.

As we've seen, our bodies cannot distinguish between a fight that's actually happening right now and one that we just keep alive by reliving it in our minds over and over again. That's why our bodies are under such great stress – not because they're actually under attack by an external source (our partner yelling at us at this moment), but because they're under attack by our own minds, our own thoughts. No negative interaction with our partners is ever really over. Our minds keep it going.

All this thinking about a fight with your partner that happened last week or even last month generates negative emotions that turn into even more thinking. You experience ever-increasing fear, anger, and hate that are toxic to your body and reap havoc on the balanced functioning of the immune system, the digestive system, the circulatory system, and the endocrine system. Holding on tight to a grudge can literally make you sick. Sometimes letting go is an act of far greater power than defending or hanging on.

> Without forgiveness, life is governed by an endless cycle of resentment and retaliation.
>
> - Robert Assagioli

The ducks teach you to 'flap your wings' – to shake off the grudge – after you've had an unpleasant interaction with your partner. Instead of carrying such a heavy burden of the past around inside of you, instead of keeping the dark cloud of negative emotions alive in your mind, sometimes for years, you can choose to focus on the only moment of power, the only moment there ever is – the *present moment*.

By letting go, you clear out some space in your mind that you use up to keep old grudges alive. And that cleared out space can then become the doorway for God to rush in and flood your life with love and peace. Stop using your anger and resentment towards your partner to block that doorway.

> To be angry about trifles is mean and churlish;
> to rage and be furious is brutish,
> and to maintain perpetual wrath
> is akin to the practice and temper of devils,
> but to prevent and suppress rising resentment
> is wise and glorious…and divine.
>
> - Isaac Watts

When you feel angry and resentful towards your partner, you remain emotionally chained to your partner. You may believe that your hurt and anger and disappointment are fully justified, but are you really prepared to carry your partner on your back for the rest of your life? When you hold a grudge against your partner, you're bound to that person by a cosmic link as real as a thick metal chain. By letting go of your grudges, you set yourself free.

> When we forgive, we set a prisoner free and discover that the person we set free is us.
>
> - Lewis Smedes

By resenting your partner, by keeping the grudge alive, you drain yourself of vital energy and give your partner complete control over your emotional well-being. That's because resentment makes you feel powerless over your own life, because your peace becomes contingent upon the words and actions of others, over which you have no control. As we'll see, forgiveness is the only solution to becoming truly free.

> When a deep injury is done us, we never recover until we forgive.
>
> - Alan Paton

7

Go Out On a Limb! Peek Over the Edge! – You Don't Need Security

> Difficult times have helped me to understand better than before
> how infinitely rich and beautiful life is in every way
> and that so many of the things one goes on worrying about
> are of no importance whatsoever.
>
> - Isak Dinesen

Divorce hits most people like an earthquake. It shakes you to the core of your being, creating a seismic shift in your life circumstances. When the thundering and tearing and shaking and rattling subside and you dare to open your eyes, the landscape is unrecognizable.

'What happened to all our plans for growing old together, having a comfortable nest egg for retirement, raising our children in the only home they've ever known, sending them to the best schools, building enduring friendships with other couples, having relationships with each other's extended family?' you ask in bewilderment? 'What happened to the life I knew, the life I so carefully planned?'

This loss of security, financial turmoil, and looming uncertainty that divorce brings, cause great suffering as you face questions such as: *Will I be able to stay in the house until the kids go off to university? Will I have to go back to work? What kind of job can I get at my age after being a stay-at-home mom for so long? How will I ever be able to afford to keep my partner and the kids in the house? How will I be able to continue to pay for private school? How am I supposed to get by on so little money? Will I ever be able to retire? How much could we get if we sold the house now, the market is so bad?*

Why do we crave security? Why do we abhor the uncertainty that divorce brings?

Because we suffer from the delusion of seeing external things – money, status, possessions, success, relationships – as the inherent source of our happiness. This delusion causes us to exaggerate the positive effect that external things can have in our lives and to want to clutch them to our chests in a death grip.

This perceived need for security and certainty results from a simple case of mistaken identity. We mistakenly believe that our egos are the totality of who we are, our entire nature.

As we'll see later, the ego is the little self we create through identification with the voice in our heads. It's the social mask we show to the world; the role we play. Divorce tends to push us deeper into the small, broken shell of our ego.

The ego is dominated by an insatiable need for more, an intense wanting.

The ego's insatiable need for more sprouts from one fundamental error – the thought: *I am not enough*. The ego needs to get more so that we can be more. 'I have therefore I am. And the more I have the more I am,' is how Eckhart Tolle describes this delusion.

If the thought of lack – whether it be financial resources or love – has become part of who you think you are (the ego), you'll always experience lack. As long as the ego remains in charge, you'll be compelled to chase after things – possessions, life circumstances, relationships – for the rest of your days in the hollow yearning for certainty and security.

It's a hollow yearning because it can never be satisfied. The ego is only ever satisfied with wanting, never with having. The satisfaction in having obtained something is short-lived. It's always quickly replaced with more wanting.

The simple truth is that nothing external will ever satisfy you, make you feel secure, make you feel contented. You'll always be looking for the next possession, person, place, or life circumstance to fill the void you feel within.

> Desire is a creature with an endless appetite.
> Like a spark put to dry grass, it just consumes.
> By its very nature it could never be satisfied
> because it is rooted in the aggression
> of looking outside of ourselves for relief.
> That expectation always results
> in disappointment, self-generated pain.
>
> - Saykong Mipham

Those who seek security chase after it for a lifetime, but it remains elusive and ephemeral, always out of reach. That's because security can never come from money or possessions alone.

The need for security is ultimately based in fear. Why fear? Because deep down we know that nothing external is permanent. Everything eventually falls away. The ego always experiences a pervasive sense of insecurity and fear because it seeks its power in impermanent things, things that are transitory.

On the other hand, when our reference point is internal, we're not afraid of challenges. We don't seek the approval of other people, and we feel neither inferior nor superior to others. This is true power – the power that is infinite and eternal. It is power based on *self-awareness*.

> Your vision will become clear only when
> you can look into your own heart.
> Who looks outside, dreams;
> who looks inside, awakens.
>
> - Carl Jung

Once you realize and accept that everything external is impermanent and will fall away as surely as it arose, you'll be at peace. You'll awaken to the dimension of the eternal within yourself.

The Waiting Game

> One of the most tragic things I know
> about human nature
> is that all of us tend to put off living.
> We are all dreaming of some magical
> rose garden over the horizon –

> instead of enjoying the roses
> blooming outside our windows today.
>
> - Dale Carnegie

Waiting is a particularly corrosive state of mind. It manifests as: *When I...,* or *If only I could...* thoughts. To you, the present moment is flawed and incomplete because some future event hasn't happened yet. You want the future. You don't want the present moment.

By being upset about what you don't have, you waste what you do have. You suffer perpetual discontent because of the inner conflict between this moment and a future moment that your mind has designed to be so much better than this moment. You suffer from the delusion of deliverance in the future.

Does this mean you shouldn't strive to improve your and your children's life circumstances after divorce? Of course not. There's nothing wrong with setting goals and working to achieve them, as long as you don't seek ultimate meaning in them.

Many people are waiting for prosperity. But prosperity cannot come in the future. Prosperity lies in the fullness of life now, in accepting the present moment, what you've got right now – and being grateful for *what is*. Acknowledging the good that's already in your life is the source of all prosperity.

> Wealth is entirely a matter of
> temperament, not of income.
> - Logan Pearsall Smith

If you focus only on what you've lost in divorce, or what you'll never have as a result of it, you're completely caught up in the smallness of the ego. The ego believes that it deserves security and certainty right now.

Soon the ego's close friend, entitlement, shows up. In the emotional turmoil caused by the ego's fear of the future and the righteous indignation stirred up by your sense of entitlement, gratitude gets trampled in the scuffle. You can't appreciate the everyday miracles and abundance of life.

If you feel frustrated or angry about the financial wasteland in which divorce has left you, you can decide to work even harder, be more ruthless, and make more money than ever before to regain your financial security. Even if you 'succeed' and recoup all the money that you had lost in divorce, or even double or triple it, the hole will still be there. The sense of lack will still be there. The undercurrent of discontent will still be there.

The sense of security that you thought money would bring you, proved to be ephemeral – it came and was gone again in the blink of an eye.

> Money may be the husk of many things,
> but not the kernel.
> It brings you food, but not appetite;
> medicine, but not health;
> acquaintances, but not friends;
> servants, but not loyalty;
> days of joy, but not peace and happiness.
>
> - Henrik Ibsen

Elizabeth Gilbert poignantly explains her own struggle:

> I have searched frantically for
> contentment for so many years in so
> many ways,
> and all these acquisitions and
> accomplishments – they run you down
> in the end.
> Life, if you keep chasing it so hard, will
> drive you to death.
> Time – when pursued like a bandit –
> will behave like one….
> At some point you have to stop because
> it won't.

> You have to admit that you can't catch it.
> That you're not supposed to catch it.
> At some point…you gotta let go and sit still and allow contentment to come to you.

You can never hope to achieve a sense of security by chasing after external things. But you can change your perspective. You can learn to turn your focus inward. That's where you'll find contentment.

Tolstoy tells the tale of an old beggar who had been sitting by the side of the road for most of his life, begging for pennies from passers-by. One day a mysterious stranger walked by. 'I don't have any money to give you,' the stranger said, 'but let me ask you: What are you sitting on?'

'Oh, just this old box,' replied the beggar. 'I've been sitting on it for forty years. It's not worth anything.' 'Look inside,' said the stranger before disappearing into the crowd.

The old beggar became intrigued. He had never opened the box. With difficulty, the old beggar managed to pry open the lid. To his utter astonishment, he found that it was filled to the brim with gold.

Many people spend their lives sitting on a chest full of gold, begging for pennies, completely unaware that their fortunes were right underneath them the whole time. They've tried to find happiness and security through all sorts of external things – power, sex, the accumulation of possessions, or money – but these things are all fleeting and disappear like mist before the dawn.

> All the wonders you seek
> are within yourself.
>
> - Thomas Browne

Your treasure is already within you. But to claim it you must break your identification with things, turn your back on the ego's wanting and yearning for security, and embrace uncertainty.

Embrace Uncertainty

> One does not discover new continents
> without consenting to lose sight of the shore
> for a very long time.
>
> - Andre Gide

The search for security is nothing other than an attachment to the known. The known is our past, the prison of past conditioning. There's absolutely no evolution in the known. And where there's no evolution, there's only stagnation, entropy, disorder, and decay.

The solution to the whole dilemma lies in the wisdom of insecurity, the wisdom of *uncertainty*. As Deepak Chopra points out, without uncertainty and the unknown, life is just the stale repetition of outworn memories. You become a victim of your past.

You're faced with a choice: You can live out your imagination or your memories; you can tie yourself to your limitless potential instead of your limiting past.

> Uncertainty and expectation are the joys of life. Security is an insipid thing.
>
> - William Congreve

Once you understand and accept the impermanence of all things, you can enjoy the external things and experiences of this world without fearing loss or dreading the future.

Divorce leads to a period of insecurity and uncertainty for almost everyone. This is because divorce involves change, and there's no change without loss. To fully protect yourself from loss would literally mean that you'd have to close the door to all of life's possibilities.

If the ego is no longer running your life, the psychological need for external security – which is illusory anyway – lessens. You become more able to live with uncertainty, even to enjoy it.

But if the ego continues to run your life, fear continues to be the predominant driver in your life. This fear prevents you from taking action or making changes in your life.

> To the timid and the hesitating
> everything is impossible
> because it seems so.
>
> - Sir Walter Scott

When you become rigidly attached to your vision of a 'secure', certain future, you shut out a whole range of possibilities. You close the door on opportunity. Through your excessive prudence you squeeze out of life all of the adventurous quality that makes it worth living.

> The desire for safety stands against every great and noble enterprise.
>
> - Tacitus

If, on the other hand, you stop looking at the world from the cramped and confining shell of your ego, if you're open to possibilities, your uncertainty will turn into increased vitality, alertness, and inspiration.

Your soul will stand ajar, ready to welcome the endless possibilities that open up in your life. You will have the courage to go out on a limb – where the plumpest, juiciest fruit are.

> Life is either a daring adventure or nothing.
>
> - Helen Keller

After my own divorce was finalized, I made the conscious choice to abandon my home, my lucrative law practice, and all my physical possessions – everything that used to give me a sense of security – and with only some clothes and a few books, I set off for another country and enrolled in graduate school. Although the lack of financial security was terrifying at times, I've never looked back.

Uncertainty is fertile ground for creativity and positive change. It's the field of untold possibilities – ever fresh, ever new. The wisdom of uncertainty is the unreserved willingness to discard the life that you've planned so as to live the life that's waiting for you.

> The important thing is this:
> to be able at any moment to sacrifice what we are
> for what we could become.

- Charles du Bos

If you're open to the possibilities, you have the wonderous ability to live the life you desire, instead of the life that landed on top of you in the earthquake that is divorce.

> The world is full of wonders and miracles,
> but man takes his little hand and covers his eyes
> and sees nothing.

- Israel Baal Shem Tov

Grounded in the wisdom of uncertainty, you can step into the unknown every moment of your life, full of excitement and anticipation.

8

What is Mindfulness?

> Our meaning comes from within.
>
> - Stephen Covey

Mindfulness is the key to escaping the divorce mindset. Mindfulness starts with the realization that when we dishonor the present moment, we suffer. As we've seen, we tend to behave unconsciously and automatically in reaction to deep-seated insecurity and fear. We are unaware of how our unexamined thoughts and emotions – especially those colored by anger, resentment, or self-pity – distort and corrupt our minds and our lives. We get stuck in the momentum of the past. We block the present moment from ever becoming a new beginning.

What is Mindfulness?

> Only that day dawns to which we are awake.
>
> - Henry David Thoreau

Divorce is a time of great inner and outer turmoil and confusion. Add to that the 'blessing' of the digital age – 24/7 connectivity that drives us to get more done in less time and allows us to get in touch with anyone, anywhere, at any time. Is it any wonder that it has become so much more difficult to get in touch with ourselves?

This is where *mindfulness* comes in. Mindfulness is about making time for yourself, about slowing down, about nurturing calmness and acceptance by experiencing the power and peace of resting in awareness in the present moment.

But above all, mindfulness is about being yourself and understanding something about who that is.

As Elizabeth Gilbert said, mindfulness is not 'some weird cryptic activity'. It's not about blissing out, experiencing ecstasy, or achieving enlightenment. It's also not about shutting out the realities of life or shutting off your mind.

Mindfulness is not dependent on any particular theoretical framework, belief system, or ideology. It's not spiritual or mystical so much as sensible. Its benefits are accessible to anyone.

Mindfulness means being awake; to walk along the path of our own lives with our eyes open, responding consciously to the world instead of reacting unconsciously to it.

Mindfulness wakes us up to the fact that our lives unfold only in moments, otherwise whole days, weeks, months, years – or even our whole lives – might slip past unnoticed. This moment is all there is – my life is *right now*. The healing power of mindfulness lies in living each moment as fully as we can.

Mindfulness is the best way to take charge of the direction and quality of our own lives, including our relationships with our partners and children, and – most fundamentally – our relationship with ourselves. The best we can do in response to the often incomprehensible and always painful life experience of divorce is to practice being at peace internally, despite the insanity that transpires around us.

In the Eye of the Storm and Twenty Feet Below the Surface

Divorce hits your life like a hurricane. Your goal should be to stay near the core – in the eye of the storm – where it's always peaceful, not at the outer edges where all the chaos and turbulence are. This core of calmness is your heart, your very being. That's where God lives inside you.

The practice of mindfulness reminds you to stop looking for answers out there in the frenzy and confusion. Mindfulness keeps bringing you back to the eye of the storm – that center that is always serene and peaceful in the midst of turmoil.

Another way of looking at mindfulness is to think of your mind as the surface of a lake (an image we've already encountered and one that we'll return to). Most of the time there are waves on the water. Sometimes the surface is only a little bit choppy; at other times there are big swells. The waves are churned up by the wind, which comes and goes, changes direction, and varies in intensity, just like the winds of stress and change in our lives which stir up the waves in our minds.

But twenty feet below the surface it's always calm, regardless of what's going on out there on the surface of the lake, whether it be a rainstorm and gale force wind or sunshine and a light breeze. Mindfulness is about staying twenty feet below the surface of your mind in that place of peace.

Mindfulness is a way of being. It's about making room for new ways of seeing old problems and coming to terms with the life situation of divorce. In this way mindfulness can make our lives more joyful and rich than they might otherwise would be. Mindfulness can restore a sense of control to us.

In short, mindfulness is about paying attention in the present moment, about being awake, and about owning our moments. It's a journey along a path that leads nowhere in particular, except to who we are.

Now that we're starting to get an idea about what mindfulness is, you might ask: 'Why should I try it? What's in it for me?'

The Benefits of Mindfulness

Eckhart Tolle compares the way in which most people go through their lives to walking along a dirt path at night, surrounded by thick fog. Luckily, you have a powerful flashlight that cuts through the fog and creates a narrow, clear space in front of you. The fog is your life situation of divorce; the flashlight is mindfulness (your conscious presence), and the clear space is the present moment.

It can be useful to admit to ourselves that many times, often at crucial times, we have no idea where we're going or even where the path lies. Mindfulness helps us to see that our lives have direction, that our lives always unfold moment by moment, and that what happens in this moment influences what's going to happen in the next.

If what happens in this moment influences what is going to happen next, doesn't it make sense for us to stop from time to time and to take our inner bearings? If we're more in touch with the present moment – with what's happening right now – we can clearly see the path that we're on and the direction in which we're moving.

Mindfulness reminds us of what there is to live for when we experience the deep personal loss and momentous change brought about by divorce – the kinds of loss and change that threaten our well-being and that of our loved ones.

What you believe you can do when going through divorce will depend entirely on how you see things, on your beliefs about your own limits and resources, and on your beliefs about life itself.

New possibilities for growth and action arise because mindfulness opens channels to deep reservoirs of creativity, clarity, determination, and wisdom within us.

When you engage in mindfulness, you don't allow your impulses – thoughts and emotions – to translate into action. You just watch them. When you don't feed, or react to, your impulses, you quickly come to realize that they almost seem to have a life of their own, that they rise and fall away, that they're not who you are but only your thoughts and emotions, and that you don't have to be ruled by them.

Mindfulness of our thoughts and feelings, particularly those that arise from our relationships with others in the stressful, threatening, and emotionally charged life situation of divorce, helps us to act effectively amid our deepest emotional pain.

As you observe the patterns of your thoughts, you will notice which areas of your life keep cropping up as distracting thoughts and pull your awareness away from the present moment. You'll easily see what you need to clear out of your 'mental closet' to be able to proceed more peacefully.

Being *Versus* Doing

> Life gives us scant time for just 'being' nowadays unless we seize it on purpose.
> - Jon Kabat-Zinn

Mostly, we run around all day long in 'doing' mode. Mindfulness is the best way to stop all the doing and to shift into 'being' mode. As we've said, mindfulness is about stopping your mental motor and being present – that's all.

The basic idea is to create an island of 'being' in the sea of constant 'doing'. By taking a few moments to 'die' to the rush of time, you free yourself to have time for the present moment. You'll notice that when you then shift from 'being' mode into 'doing' mode once again, it's a different kind of doing for having stopped. The stopping helps to keep all the things we worry about and feel inadequate about in perspective.

> Practice stopping, sitting down,
> and becoming aware of your breathing
> once in a while during the day –
> be it for five minutes or five seconds.

When you're immersed in 'doing' without being mindful, you feel like you're away from home. When you reconnect with 'being', even if only for a few moments, you experience a familiar feeling of 'wholeness'. It's a deeply familiar memory that is suppressed by the mind's usual agitation and reactivity. However, when you reconnect with 'being', you recognize the feeling of 'wholeness' immediately. You feel at home regardless of where you are and regardless of the problems that you face.

Be Where You Are

> If you let yourself be blown to and fro,
> you lose touch with your root.
> If you let restlessness move you,
> you lose touch with who you are.
>
> - Lao-Tsu

Once I went hiking with friends in the mountains of Lesotho, a small kingdom in Southern Africa. About an hour after we set out one morning, a blanket of dense fog descended over the mountains.

We could barely see each other, let alone the trail that we were supposed to follow. Instead of staying put until the fog lifted, we soldiered on. By late morning, when the sun started burning off the fog, we were hopelessly lost.

As we rounded a bend, we came across an old man sitting in front of his hut, enjoying the sunshine. 'Old father, can you tell us where we are?' one of my friends asked. The old man looked puzzled for a moment, and then replied: 'You are here, of course.' We were all dumbstruck by this profound wisdom.

Being mindful means to commit fully in each moment to being present. Mindfulness is the only intentional human activity which is not fundamentally about trying to improve yourself or get anywhere else, but simply to realize where you already are.

The spirit of mindfulness means to take each moment as it comes – pleasant, unpleasant, good, bad, or ugly – and work with it, because that's what is present right now.

> What lies behind us and
> what lies before us
> are tiny matters compared to
> what lies within us.
>
> - Oliver Wendell Holmes

When we turn inward for some part of each day, we connect with what's most real and most reliable – but also most easily overlooked – in ourselves.

When we are centered in ourselves, even for brief periods of time, in the face of the push and pull of the external world, we can be at home wherever we find ourselves. We can be at peace with things as they are, moment by moment.

So why don't you simply let go and admit that you might as well be at home wherever you are?

Try the following experiment: The next time you feel dissatisfied with something or someone, or even when you just experience a vague sense of dissatisfaction, turn inward. Instead of calling a friend, checking your social media feeds, picking up a magazine, turning on the television, or looking for something to eat, see if you can just sit quietly and 'be' with that very moment.

> Just sit.
> Be where you are.
> Let things be as they are.

Be Strong Enough to be Weak

Divorce is often a time when you face an *impasse* in your life. You're unable to go forward, to turn around, or to go back. You're practically forced to stop and contemplate your life, to question who you are and where to find meaning in your life's journey.

At such times it's so easy to blame, to find fault, to become imprisoned by the belief that the cause of your suffering lies out there – with your partner, or the judge, or the downturn in the economy, or the slow court system – but never within yourself. You look for an escape from the forces that you perceive to be holding you back and preventing you from finding happiness.

But, as you've probably realized by now, there's no escaping your current life situation of divorce. Sooner or later, everything that you don't want to deal with or that you pretend aren't there and that you try to escape from, catch up to you.

The reason is simply that you carry your head and your heart with you everywhere you go. When you get to the beach or the retreat or the bar or wherever else you try to flee to, there you would be, with the same head and the same heart.

Sooner or later the same problems surface, because they stem largely from your old patterns of thinking and behaving. In the long run there's no escaping from ourselves. There can be only transformation. When we're not able to change our life circumstances, we're challenged to change ourselves.

In divorce we tend to be so defensive against feeling the impact of our emotional pain – whether it be grief, sadness, shame, disappointment, or anger – that we unconsciously escape into a cocoon of numbness in which we don't permit ourselves to feel anything at all or to examine what we're feeling.

There can be no resolution and growth until you fully face this moment – this place, this relationship, this dilemma. The challenge of mindfulness is to work with the moment you find yourself in, no matter how painful, discouraging, or limiting it may be.

For mindfulness to do its work, you must be willing to do yours. You must be willing to face – even embrace – darkness and despair, over and over again if need be, without attempting to escape or numbing yourself in the multitude of ways people try to avoid the unavoidable.

> We don't receive wisdom.
> We must discover it for ourselves
> after a journey that no one can take
> for us or spare us.
>
> - Marcel Proust

It's especially in times of great emotional turmoil, anger, grief, and fear in which you feel rejected, vulnerable, hurt, lost, humiliated, or defeated – that you need reassurance that the core of your being is stable and resilient, and that it rests in the eye of storm.

Working mindfully with your thoughts and emotions starts by acknowledging to yourself what you're actually feeling or thinking about in the present moment. It is helpful to completely stop, even for a short time, and simply sit with your hurt – breathing with it, experiencing it fully without trying to change it or explain it away. The idea is to observe your emotional pain as it unfolds, with openness and acceptance. This brings calmness.

Whatever you feel at this moment – grief, sadness, or anything else – try just letting it be there.

> Allow yourself to just feel whatever you're feeling in this moment.

All that's required for mindfulness is a willingness to be awake to your present moments, no matter what they hold, in a spirit of kindness and generosity to yourself and openness to what might be possible.

9

How to Practice Mindfulness

As we've seen in the previous chapter, mindfulness is the process of observing our minds intentionally, of letting our thoughts and emotions unfold from moment to moment and *accepting them as they are*, without rejecting them or trying to suppress them.

It's only when our minds are open and receptive that learning, seeing, and change can occur.

Simple, But Not Easy

From the outside, the practice of mindfulness seems pretty simple:

1. You just sit quietly and comfortably – on the floor or on a chair, whatever is most comfortable for you.

2. You breathe consciously. That means putting all your attention on the movement of your breath as it enters through your nostrils and moves into your chest and abdomen, and then following the breath along the same path out as you exhale.

Thich Nhat Hanh describes the practice of mindfulness as cloudy apple juice settling in a glass: 'You just sit…the mind settles itself.'

However, the practice of mindfulness might be simple in concept, but it's difficult in execution. In the beginning, I found it very challenging. Almost immediately after sitting down, I felt a general sense of agitation. I noticed that my mind wasn't calm at all. It was, as Elizabeth Gilbert describes, like a 'zippy fish, darting this way and that'.

I soon realized that I spent shockingly little time in the present moment. I regretted or waxed nostalgic for things that happened in the past, or I worried about or wished for things that might come to pass in the future. Whole stretches of time went by during which I flew off on mental tangents and completely forgot that I was sitting in a chair in my study trying to be mindful.

You can easily observe for yourself the mind's tendency to escape from the present moment. Just try to keep your attention focused on any object – a mug, a pen, anything in your immediate vicinity – for even s short period of time.

You'll quickly realize that to cultivate mindfulness, you'll have to remind yourself over and over again to be awake and aware.

> If your mind isn't clouded by unnecessary things, this is the best season of life.
>
> - Wu-Men

We habitually and unconsciously waste enormous amounts of energy in reacting to the outside world and to our own thoughts and emotions. Cultivating mindfulness means learning to tap into and focus our own wasted energies.

It's helpful to think of mindfulness as a lens that focuses the scattered and reactive energies of our minds into an efficient source of energy for problem solving and for living.

Obstacles

Our thinking minds are undoubtedly the biggest obstacle along the journey of mindfulness. Practicing mindfulness involves repeatedly bringing your attention back to the present moment.

But 'paying attention' doesn't mean 'thinking about'. 'Paying attention' means just letting your experience unfold as it does and being aware of the process. You just watch all images, thoughts, and sensations arise and pass away, without being bothered by them, without reacting to them, without labelling them, or without judging them.

Mindfulness is also not 'relaxation' spelled differently. If you do a relaxation exercise and you're still stressed out after you're done, you've failed. But if you practice mindfulness, then the only important thing is whether you're willing to look at the present moment as it is – including discomfort, tension, or feelings of failure or fear. If you are, then you haven't failed.

As you sit mindfully, don't try to stop thinking. If you try to stop thinking, it means you're bothered by thinking. Don't be bothered by anything.

It only seems as if thoughts that arise come from outside your mind, but they're actually just waves of your mind. If you don't let them bother you, gradually the waves will become calmer and calmer. If you learn to simply watch your thoughts go past, your mind will come to a natural place of rest. Your mental motor will eventually stop by itself.

Leaves Floating Down a Stream

A helpful image to keep you from getting lost in your thoughts is to see your thoughts as autumn leaves floating down a stream. The leaves drift by, moved this way and that by the swirling water. Focus on the stream, not the leaves.

Your mind may dwell on a memory, an image, a sound, or any of a thousand things. When you notice your mind clinging to any of these 'leaves', very gently bring it back to the stream.

Don't get angry or frustrated because your attention got caught up in a thought, because that anger or frustration is just another leaf.

Don't try to fight off thoughts or emotions. Just watch them float past and let them go.

Your attention will get caught up a thousand times. Each time, very gently but firmly bring it back to the flowing water.

Why Do We Focus on Our Breathing?

Because our minds tend to behave like 'zippy fish', it helps to have a focus for our attention when we practice mindfulness, an anchor line that tethers us to the present moment and guides us back when our minds wander. Our breathing is that anchor.

We use our breath as an 'object' to focus on during mindfulness practice precisely because it's not an object at all; it has no shape or form. Because the breath has no form, it has since ancient times been associated with spirit.

> God formed man of dust from the ground
> and breathed into his nostrils the breath of life
> and the man became a living creature.
>
> - Genesis 2:7

Our modern word 'breath' is derived from the Latin 'spiritus', which simultaneously means 'breath' and 'spirit'. In Eastern traditions 'breath' relates to the Sanskrit word 'atman', meaning the 'indwelling divine spirit', or 'God within'.

Being aware of our breath forces us into the present moment – the only place where transformation can take place. That's because breathing disentangles us from the compulsive and habitual hold of the mind.

Whenever we are conscious of our breath, we are present. It's impossible to be aware of your mind *and* of your breathing. Conscious breathing stops the mental motor. Giving our minds one thing to be aware of – the breath – replaces a plethora of things that our minds usually find to preoccupy themselves with.

Focusing on our breathing also increases our powers of concentration. Our minds become calmer and more focused. Then we're able to be aware of our thoughts and emotions with a more discerning eye. We're able to see our life situation more clearly and with greater perspective – all because we're more awake, more aware.

With this awareness comes a feeling of spaciousness, of having more 'room to breathe', of having more options, of being free to choose effective responses in stressful situations, rather than losing our equilibrium and becoming reactive to our own thoughts and outside pressures.

If we can realize the fullness of *this* moment – of *this* breath – we can find peace right here and now. We can be home in *this* moment as it is.

> God Himself culminates
> in the present moment,
> and will never be more divine,
> in the lapse of all the ages.
>
> - Thoreau, *Walden*

How to Breathe Mindfully

Close your eyes and bring your attention to the motion of your breath as it enters and leaves your body. Just focus on the feeling of it, the feeling of the breath coming into your body and the feeling of the breath leaving your body.

| Just feel the breath. That's all.

'Paying attention' to your breathing means just that – paying attention, like a doorman watching each person coming and going through a door – with alert, dispassionate attention. Nothing more.

Don't try to change anything about your breathing. Don't start to breathe more deeply, or force your breath, or try to change the pattern or rhythm of your breathing.

Don't worry whether you're doing it right. Trust me, you're doing it right. Your breath has been moving in and out of your body for all your life without you having given it much thought.

Try to stay with one full inbreath as it comes in and one full outbreath as it goes out. Let go of any ideas about getting somewhere or having anything happen.

As you've probably noticed, focusing and staying with your breath is easier said than done. Lots of thoughts intrude or carry us off.

Our minds have become cluttered over the years, like an attic, with lots of accumulated junk. Just this knowledge is already a big step in the right direction.

Your thinking mind will drift to and fro on the currents and winds moving your mind until, at some point, the anchor line draws taught and brings you back to your breathing.

This might happen a lot. No worries. Just bring your attention back to your breathing every time your mind wanders.

There are several places in the body where you can observe your breath. You can feel the breath as it flows past your nostrils, or in your chest as it expands on each inbreath and contracts on each outbreath, or in your belly as it moves in and out with each breath.

I personally find focusing on my breath at my belly to be particularly calming. It reminds me of the image of mindfulness as a lake. Just as the surface of the lake can be choppy when the wind is blowing, so, too, can my mind be reactive and agitated when my outside circumstances are not calm and peaceful, or I just have 'a lot on my mind'.

But twenty feet down the lake is calm even if the surface is agitated. Similarly, when I focus on my breathing down in my belly, I feel like I'm tuning in to a part of my body that is below the agitations of my thinking mind and is intrinsically calmer, more relaxed, and more stable.

Set Aside Some Quiet Time Every Day

> All of humanity's problems
> stem from man's inability
> to sit quietly in a room.
>
> - Pascal

I know that in the chaos and complexity of divorce, with all its demands and responsibilities and frustrations, it can be difficult to carve out some time to sit quietly in mindfulness.

But I don't know anyone whom I consider to be inwardly peaceful who doesn't carve out at least a little quiet time almost every day. Quiet time to yourself is a vital part of life.

A quiet mind is the foundation for inner peace. And inner peace translates into outer peace.

> Try to set some time aside each day for mindfulness.
> Five minutes is enough –
> ten or twenty or thirty, if possible, would be great.
> Just sit and watch the moment with no agenda –
> other than to be fully present.

Mindfulness in Daily Life

Needless to say, we don't have complete control over all aspects of our lives. But it's also true that we're so often driven, not by an outside circumstance that requires us to hurry, but by our self-created, inner hurry fueled by mindless, anxious thinking.

That's why it's so important to slow down with mindful intention, whenever possible. This adds an element of deep freedom to our lives, a freedom which so easily eludes us if we don't seek it consciously.

Luckily, there are many opportunities – even amidst the hurly-burly of family life and work – to bring moment-to-moment awareness to the tasks, experiences, and encounters of ordinary living – such as setting the table, eating, doing the laundry, vacuuming the carpet, taking out the garbage, mowing the lawn, brushing our teeth, taking a shower, cleaning out the garage, riding a bike, taking the train, getting on a bus, or talking on the phone.

You can intentionally slow down by doing one thing at a time and making sure that you're present for that one thing. When you spend time with your child, consciously tell your mind and your body to *be with* your child, rather than automatically reaching for your phone, or turning on the television.

You can also make the conscious choice to sit and do nothing for an entire evening, or to read a book, or to go for a walk alone or with your child, or to look at the moon, or to feel a breeze on your face, or to go to bed early. Whatever you do, be present in mind and body for the activity.

> See if you can use ordinary, repetitive tasks in your home
> as invitations to practice mindfulness.

I found doing the dishes to be a great opportunity for practicing mindfulness. I came to see that I don't have to rush to get through the dishes so that I can get to something more important, because during those moments that I'm doing the dishes, that *is* my life.

It dawned on me that the whole point was to really *do* the dishes when I was doing them, to be aware as I was doing the dishes, mindful of the tendency to slip into autopilot and do them unconsciously.

This shift in my perspective transformed an annoying chore into a mindful experience.

> No drives, no compulsions,
> no needs, no attractions —
> then your affairs
> are under control.
> You are free.

- Thomas Merton

10

The Pillars of Mindfulness – Surrender to Life

> Whatever you fight, you strengthen, and whatever you resist, persists.
>
> - Eckhart Tolle

Now that we have a better understanding of what mindfulness is and how we can practice mindfulness, we now turn to the pillars of mindfulness. The first of these pillars is *surrender*.

Surrender or *acceptance* or *non-resistance* is the simple but profound wisdom of yielding to the flow of life rather than resisting it.

Surrender means to let things be, to accept things as they are. It's about seeing yourself as larger than your problems and your pain.

Surrender means to stop clinging to anything – an idea of what marriage ought to be, a relationship that is over, a particular time when you thought you were 'happy', a desire for things to be different, feelings of being overwhelmed, discouraged, or hopeless.

Surrender means to stop resisting and struggling. It means to make room for something more powerful and wholesome in your life by allowing things to be as they are, without getting caught up in your attraction to or rejection of external circumstances.

Surrender is akin to letting your palm open to release something you've been holding on to.

> The bird of paradise
> alights only upon the hand that does not grasp.
>
> - John Berry

If you're one of the thousands of people who find the life situation of divorce unsatisfactory or even intolerable, it's only by surrendering first that you can break the pattern of resistance that often makes the situation worse.

That's because, as we've seen, it's the quality of your consciousness in this moment that determines to the greatest degree what kind of future you will experience.

To surrender is the most important thing you can do to bring about positive change in your life.

If your overall life situation – divorce – is unpleasant, surrender to *what is* in this particular moment. In other words, surrender in each moment to the reality of that moment.

What is cannot be undone because it already *is as it is*. So, you say 'yes' to what is and accept what is not. Then you do what the situation requires.

When the pain of divorce is deep, you'll likely have a strong urge to escape it rather than to surrender to it. That's perfectly normal. There are many pseudo escapes – work, drink, drugs, sex, anger, suppression. But, ultimately, there is no escape; there is no way out.

Surrendering is especially difficult when you've been betrayed, abandoned, or deceived. But until you surrender, you'll be glued to the pain of your divorce.

When you resist or deny your emotional pain, it contaminates everything you think and do. Your perceptions become distorted and selective; you only see what you want to see and then you misinterpret what you see.

Even if you cannot see a way out of your emotional pain, there is still a way *through*. But this requires that you don't try to escape the pain. Rather, face the grief, despair, fear, loneliness, or whatever form your emotional pain takes. Don't resist it. Allow it to be there. Make no mistake, this takes courage.

'Feeling' your pain doesn't mean 'thinking about' it. 'Feeling' it simply means witnessing it without labelling it mentally. Give all your attention to the feeling itself, not to the person or event that you believe caused your emotional pain. As you feel the pain, realize fully that at this moment, this is what you feel. There's nothing you can do about the fact that at this moment, this is what you feel.

> There is no arguing with the inevitable.
> The only argument available with an east wind
> is to put on your coat.
>
> - James Russell Lowell

Wanting this moment – the shock, the disbelief, the fear, the anger – to be different from what it is just adds more emotional pain to the pain you're already experiencing.

But the moment you stop identifying with the feeling of emotional pain, the moment you put your attention on it directly, it can no longer control your thinking.

> If you let yourself be absorbed completely, if you surrender completely to the moments as they pass, you live more richly in those moments.

- Anne Morrow Lindberg

Whatever you cannot enjoy doing – interacting with your ex-in-laws, seeing your partner at a school concert, or whatever other unpleasant thing divorce requires of you – you can at least accept.

Acceptance says: *For now, this is what the situation requires me to do, so I do it willingly. I accept this moment completely.*

> Acceptance is the answer to all my problems today…
> I can find no serenity until I accept
> that person, place, thing, or situation
> as being exactly the way it is supposed to be at this moment.

- Alcoholics Anonymous

You don't want to stand rigid like the tall oak that cracks and collapses in the storm. Instead, you want to be flexible like the willow that bends with the storm and survives.

> Today I know I cannot control the ocean tides.
> I can only go with the flow...
> When I struggle and try to organize the Atlantic
> to my specifications,
> I sink.
> If I flail and thrash and growl and rumble,
> I go under.
> But if I let go and float,
> I am borne aloft.
>
> - Marie Stilkind

Make this commitment to yourself every day:

> Today, I will accept all people, situations,
> circumstances, and events
> as they occur,
> because I know every moment is as it should be.

As we experience the life situation of divorce, we often waste enormous amounts of energy denying or resisting what is already the case. When we deny or resist, we try to force situations to be the way we want them to be. This only creates more tension, more suffering, and it prevents positive change.

> Our limited perspective, our hopes, and fears become our measure of life, and when circumstances don't fit our ideas, they become our difficulties.
>
> - Benjamin Franklin

Life is rarely the way we would like it to be. Life is simply the way it is. The greater our surrender to the present moment, the greater will be our sense of peace.

You're much more likely to know what to do, and to have the inner conviction to act, when you have a clear picture of what's actually happening, than when your vision is clouded by your mind's self-serving judgments and desires and fears and prejudices.

The mindful view is that only through surrendering to the present moment – no matter how painful or frightening or undesirable it may be – can change and growth and healing come about.

In this way, we take each moment as it comes, we see it clearly in its fullness, we accept it, and then we let it go.

Is That So?

A wise man lived in a small town. One day, the wise man's neighbor arrived at his door. 'My daughter is pregnant, and she says you're the father!' the man yelled and accusingly pointed his finger at the wise man.

'Is that so?' was all the wise man replied.

The wise man's neighbor told everyone in the village what the wise man had done. One day the mayor arrived at the wise man's door and said: 'Your reputation is ruined. We don't want you to preside over the harvest festival this year.'

'Is that so?' was all the wise man replied.

When the baby was born, the neighbor brought the infant to the wise man and said: 'I'm leaving the baby here. You have to take care of it.'

'Is that so?' was all that the wise man replied.

For more than a year the wise man lovingly fed and nurtured the baby and took care of all its needs. One day the neighbor showed up at the wise man's door. With his cap in hand the neighbor said: 'I'm really sorry. My daughter confessed that you're not the father. The baby's father is the grocer's son. I came to take back the baby.'

'Is that so?' was all the wise man replied before handing the baby back to his neighbor.

The wise man responds to bad news and good news and false accusations and truth in exactly the same way. 'Is that so?' is his only response. He accepts the present moment exactly as it is.

When you fully accept what happens, what happens doesn't have any power over you anymore. But if you resist what happens, you're at the mercy of what happens. Then external circumstances will determine your happiness and unhappiness.

When Gandhi was shot at point-blank range, he put his palms together as a sign of forgiveness towards his attacker, he uttered his mantra, and then he died. Gandhi was able to bring the perspective of surrender to every aspect of his life, including his very life. Surrender allowed him to choose the attitude he would assume in the very moment that he was being robbed of life.

What Surrender is Not

Surrender doesn't mean 'resignation' – passively putting up with whatever circumstances you find yourself in or abandoning your principles.

An attitude of 'I just don't care anymore' is tainted with hidden resentment, which is not surrender at all, but is in fact masked resistance.

If you resist what is – the 'suchness of life', as the Buddha called it – you make yourself and your loved ones suffer, and many times you don't even realize that you're doing it.

When difficulties arise – when the court hearing doesn't go as planned, when their partners refuse to be cooperative – instead of immediately accepting the situation, many people resist and react against the situation. They feel personally offended and resentful. All their protests and anger burn up a huge amount of energy – energy that could be used to solve the problem.

What's more, this negative energy creates more resistance, more obstacles, and more opposition. For example, if you resist your partner's upsetting communications, then he/she will keep trying to communicate the same things over and over again until he/she is heard.

We live with the illusion that the 'shield' of resistance will somehow protect us from feeling the loss, guilt, distress, or anguish of our current life situation of divorce. But resistance is nothing other than weakness and fear masquerading as strength.

Surrender also doesn't necessarily mean 'doing nothing'. Surrender is perfectly compatible with making plans, taking action, or initiating change. But in the surrendered state, a different quality, a different energy flows into your doing. Eckhart Tolle calls this *'surrendered action'*. In the surrendered state, you can see very clearly what needs to be done and then you take action.

Ask yourself:

> Is there anything I can do to change the situation,
> to improve it,
> or to remove myself from it?

If there is something you can do, take appropriate action. If there is nothing you can do, say to yourself: *Right now, this is how it is. I can either accept it or make myself miserable.*

Take responsibility for your life.

11

The Pillars of Mindfulness – Non-Judgment and Non-Attachment

Non-Judgment

When we practice mindfulness, it doesn't take long to discover that our minds are constantly evaluating and judging our thoughts and emotions. When we constantly evaluate, classify, label, and analyze, we create a lot of turbulence in our inner dialogue.

This turbulence leads to fear – fear that we're not good enough, fear that bad things will happen, fear that good things won't last, and fear that people might hurt us.

Our mental habit of judging our thoughts and emotions makes it difficult for us to ever be at peace. The mind is like a yo-yo, Jon Kabat-Zinn reminds us, going up and down on the string of our own judging thoughts all day long.

This judgmental thinking also weighs down the mind. It's like carrying a hiker's full backpack. After a long, hot day trekking up mountains and down valleys, it's such a physical relief to let the backpack just drop to the ground.

It feels just as liberating mentally to suspend all of our judging and instead letting each moment be just as it is, without attempting to label it 'good' or 'bad'.

We say to ourselves: *Pleasure and pain, loss and gain, fame, and shame, are all the same. They're neither good nor bad. They're just happening.*

What follows is peace.

'Maybe So, Maybe Not'

Because all things and events are deeply interconnected, the mental labels of 'good' and 'bad' are ultimately illusory. They always imply a limited perspective.

This is illustrated by the story of a wise woman who was approached by her neighbor one day. The neighbor said: 'A terrible thing has happened. My ox died and now I have no animal to help me plough my field. Isn't this the worst thing that could possibly have happened?'

'Maybe so, maybe not,' the wise woman replied. The neighbor returned home furious at the wise woman's attitude.

He told his family that the wise woman must have lost her mind.

The very next day the neighbor was back at the wise woman's door. 'You won't believe what happened,' the neighbor said, 'this morning when I woke up, I saw a horse grazing in my garden. I asked around, but the horse didn't belong to anyone. So, I harnessed the horse and ploughed my field. It went even faster than with my old ox. Don't you think this is the best stroke of luck?'

'Maybe so, maybe not,' the wise woman replied. The neighbor returned home perplexed, even more convinced that the wise woman had lost her mind.

A few days later the neighbor returned to the wise woman. 'Yesterday my son was thrown from our new horse, and he broke his leg,' the neighbor complained. 'Who's going to help me with the harvest this year? We will surely starve to death! Isn't this the worst news ever?'

'Maybe so, maybe not,' the wise woman responded.

'I don't know why I tell you anything!' yelled the neighbor, as he stormed off in a huff.

Two days later the neighbor was at the wise woman's door again. He said to the wise woman: 'The emperor's troops arrived yesterday and conscripted all the young men to fight in the war. My son was the only one in the village not dragged off to certain death. Am I not just the most fortunate father in the whole world?'

'Maybe so, maybe not,' the wise woman responded. The neighbor left, more perplexed than ever.

The wise woman's 'maybe so, maybe not' signifies a refusal to judge anything that happens. The wise woman demonstrates to her neighbor that, instead of judging, he should accept the present moment as it presents itself.

The wise woman knows that it's often impossible to understand what purpose a seemingly random event has in the tapestry of the whole. That's because there are no random events. The causes of even the smallest events are virtually infinite and relate to the whole in incomprehensible ways.

Don't approach the world with a set of expectations and beliefs and preconceptions. Stay open. See every moment with fresh eyes. Shunryu Suzuki calls this essential approach to life *'beginner's mind'*.

The approach we take in mindfulness is to witness thoughts and emotions as they come up in our minds, without condemning them or pursuing them. This doesn't mean that you'll stop judging your thoughts. It's in the very nature of the mind to compare and to judge and to evaluate.

When you find your mind judging your thoughts and emotions, don't try to stop it from doing that. There is no need to judge the judging, or to act on your judging thoughts and emotions and make matters even more complicated for yourself. To find a more effective way of handling the stress of divorce, all that's required is to be aware that it's happening.

When you sit mindfully with your doubts, fears, and problems, your judgmental attitude towards them tends to dissolve over time. You come to see what you need to know or do. What seemed impenetrable or murky becomes clear.

The way to handle thoughts (the judgmental or any other kind), is simply to observe them as thoughts, to be aware of them as passing events in the field of your consciousness without getting caught up in them.

Of course, we're not only judgmental about ourselves and our own thoughts. We also judge, criticize, and blame other people, often those closest to us.

Judging and finding fault with others take a great deal of energy and, without exception, pulls us away from where we want to be.

That's why it's helpful to try having a non-judging perspective towards the ways in which other people behave. This helps us to become more compassionate and more patient.

To paraphrase a popular psychology book from the 90s, we recognize that 'I'm not okay, you're not okay, and that's okay'.

A non-judging orientation certainly doesn't mean that we stop knowing how to act responsibly, or that we condone everything that someone else says or does.

It simply means that we can act with much greater clarity in our own lives and be more balanced, more effective, and more ethical in how we engage with the world.

Non-Attachment

> Weeping may endure for a night,
> but joy cometh in the morning.
>
> - Psalm 30:5

I ran into a former client in the supermarket several years after her divorce. I asked her how she was doing. She said: 'Even now, although I think of Chris less often, when I'm crossing the street or drifting off to sleep perhaps, I'm suddenly hit with a pang of profound loss. That brief thought leads to great sadness.'

If you're going through a divorce right now, I know that you, too, often feel sad. But when we hold on to the way things used to be, or the way we want them to remain, we suffer.

We ignore the evidence we see all around us every day. *Impermanence* is the way of life – everything that arises eventually falls away.

Physicists have discovered that the apparent solidity of matter is an illusion created by our senses. Even what we think of as inanimate material objects are subject to continuous change. Rocks, mountains, continents, earth itself, and even stars and galaxies all change over time. They arise and they fall away.

Because we humans live for such a short period of time compared to these things, we tend to think of them as permanent, unchanging. But they're not. Nothing is.

Whether we like it or not, change is all around us. Change is absolutely normal. We're the ones who add all the fear and drama. Change, and even death, just *are.* There's no point in fighting them. An old Buddhist teaching holds:

> The world is afflicted with death and decay, therefore the wise do not grieve, knowing the terms of the world.

The thoughts and feelings that arise in divorce are so powerful that they often seem overwhelming. But they don't have to be so powerful. Over time, you'll see that – like everything else in life – these thoughts and feelings are *impermanent*. They rise up, completely occupy your mind for a while, then drift away.

When practicing mindfulness, direct your attention *on* and *into* your emotional pain, no matter how bad it seems. After all, it is what you're feeling right now, so you might as well see if you can accept it, at least a little bit.

As you try to be mindful and calm with your emotional pain, it can be a great comfort to know that the hurt, the discomfort, or whatever you're experiencing in that moment is *not permanent*. As these troublesome thoughts and emotions arise, they will fall away again.

If you can assume this attitude of calm, non-attached awareness of your emotional pain – for one breath or even just half a breath at first – that's a step in the right direction.

If you learn to see change as an integral and inescapable part of life – and not as a threat to your well-being – you will be in a much better position to cope with the life situation of divorce; you will live with a much lighter heart.

'This, Too, Shall Pass'

According to an ancient story there was a king who was constantly torn between happiness and despondency. The slightest thing could send him flying off into a rage or into a dark pit of despair.

One day a wise person arrived at the king's court. The king told the wise person of his suffering and that he was tired of himself and the way he lived. He asked the wise person: 'Is there a way to bring balance, serenity, and wisdom into my life?'

The wise person reached into a satchel and brought out a plain-looking ring without precious stones or other adornments. 'This ring is more valuable than all the gold and jewels in your kingdom', the wise person said, handing the ring to the king.

On the ring was an inscription: *This, too, shall pass.*

'What does it mean?' asked the king.

The wise person replied: 'Wear this ring always. No matter what happens, before you call it good or bad, touch the ring and read the inscription. Then you will always be at peace.'

Be Grateful When You're Feeling Good and Gracious When You're Feeling Bad

We've all experienced that our moods can be extremely deceptive. They often trick us into believing that life is far worse than it actually is.

When we're feeling low – anxious, depressed, tired – life seems serious and difficult. We have no perspective. We take things personally and often impute malignant motives to the people around us and so misinterpret what they say and do.

The difference between a peaceful person and someone who is not at peace, isn't how often they experience low moods or even how low their moods get. Instead, it's what they do with their low moods, how they relate to their changing feelings.

There comes a time in every person's life when he/she feels low. But to peaceful people this is just the way of things. They understand that moods are an unavoidable human condition that *will pass in time*; both good (positive) and bad (negative) moods come and go.

When peaceful people feel depressed, angry, stressed, or fearful, they relate to their feelings with openness and wisdom. Rather than panic because they're experiencing a low mood or try to fight their feelings – which just strengthens the bad feelings – they accept their feelings, resting in the knowledge that this, too, shall pass.

Rather than fight negative feelings, positive people are gracious in their acceptance of these negative feelings. It's almost as if they say to themselves: *This is no big deal, because when the time is right, I'll be at peace again.* This allows them to come gently and gracefully out of negative feeling states into more positive states of mind.

> Grief and nuisance are inevitable in this life, but if you can plant yourself in stillness long enough, you will, in time, experience the truth that everything (both uncomfortable and lovely) does eventually pass.
>
> - Elizabeth Gilbert

The fundamental truth is that life is constructed in such a way that if we wish to enjoy its pleasures, we must also be prepared to endure its pains. Whether we like it or not, we can't have one without the other. We might as well accept it.

When you feel discouraged, depressed, or lonely, remind yourself that these feelings will pass, and that you will again experience joy, pleasure, fulfilment, and peace.

A perspective of non-attachment doesn't mean being uninvolved; it means being involved without attachment. Non-attachment doesn't mean you ignore your painful thoughts and emotions; it means you feel them fully, but without getting caught up in them.

Non-attachment is like untangling a net without getting caught up in the net yourself. Attachment to your thoughts and feelings is like trying to untangle a net but getting caught in the net – before long, what was a simple task of untangling becomes a life-and-death struggle.

Non-attachment also doesn't interfere with setting goals. You can still have the intention of going in a certain direction, to move towards your goal, but you don't get attached to either the direction or the goal.

You realize that between the point of departure and the destination, there are infinite possibilities. With the perspective that non-attachment brings, you might change direction at any moment if you find a higher ideal or something more worthwhile. You are also less likely to force solutions on problems, which enables you to stay alert to opportunities.

The story of the wise man whose only response was, 'Is that so?' shows the good that comes from inner non-resistance to events, the wisdom of surrendering to life. The story of the wise woman whose only comment on her neighbor's travails was a pointed, 'Maybe so, maybe not' illustrates the wisdom of non-judgment. The story of the ring points to the fact of impermanence, the inevitability of change, which leads to an attitude of non-attachment.

Non-resistance, *non-judgment*, and *non-attachment* are the three pillars of mindfulness that lead to true freedom.

12

Ego and Self-Awareness

> Like two golden birds perched on the self-same tree, intimate friends, the ego and the Self dwell in the same body. The former eats the sweet and sour fruits of the tree of life, while the latter looks on in detachment.
>
> - The Mundaka Upanishad

Ego

As we grow up, we form a mental image of who we are. This mental image is based on our personal and cultural conditioning. It's our social mask, the role we play for others. This mental image of ourselves is called the 'ego'.

The ego thrives on approval, control, and power because it's fundamentally based in fear. It's that part of us that wants to be seen, heard, respected, and adored, often at the expense of someone else.

The most important thing to know about the ego is that it consists entirely of mind activity. It came into existence, and it can only be kept going, through constant thinking.

The more that you identify with your mind, with thinking, the denser your ego becomes. The denser the ego is in you, the more likely it is that you perceive other people to be the main source of problems in your life.

Some people enjoy brief periods of freedom from the ego, for example when they first arrive at a new destination, when they see breathtaking natural beauty or a beautiful painting, when they take a bite of delicious food, or when they are in the throes of sexual ecstasy. The peace, joy, and aliveness that they experience in those moments make life worth living.

Other people are constantly trapped in their egos. They are alienated from themselves, from other people, and from the world around them. Alienation means that they never feel at ease in any circumstance, at any place, or with any person, least of all with themselves. They always try to get 'home', but they never feel 'at home'.

Alienated people who are trapped in their egos are not present in any life situation. Their attention is always either in the past (rerunning the old movies of their lives) or in the future (being plagued by fearful scenarios that might never occur) – which exists only in the mind as thoughts.

The ego can simply be understood as the unobserved mind that runs your life when you are not present.

Struggle, stress, or negative reactions when you encounter obstacles are signs that your ego is active.

The ego convinces you not just that you need it, but that you *are* it. This is how the ego tries to stay in charge. It keeps you feeling separate; it tries to convince you that you're flawed and broken and alone.

The ego doesn't want to serve you. All it wants is to stay in power, to assert its authority by playing with your mind. It wants to keep you cornered off from the rest of the universe.

Divorce pushes you deeper into the small, broken shell of the ego. One of the most important lessons to learn in divorce is to stop looking at life from the narrow, disconnected, discontented perspective of the ego.

You need a shift in perspective that allows you to choose from a place where you're empowered rather than disempowered.

'I', 'Me' and 'Mine'

> The true value of a human being is determined primarily by the measure and sense in which he has attained liberation from the self [ego].
>
> - Albert Einstein

'Selfing' is the inevitable tendency of the mind to construct an 'I', 'me', or 'mine' out of almost everything and out of almost every situation – and then to operate in life from that limited perspective.

See if you can watch your thoughts and feelings as just thoughts and feelings. Do you catch yourself identifying with them as 'my' thoughts, 'my' feelings, 'my' anger, 'my' anxiety? Let go of the 'my' and just accept this moment as it is.

When we look deeply into our emotional pain, we see the constellation of thoughts and feelings – the reacting, the judging, the rejecting of how we feel at this moment, and the wishing to feel something different – that are going on in our minds.

It took me a long time to realize that 'I am not my emotional pain', unless I go along with the ego's identification with the emotional pain, unless I make it 'my' emotional pain. Maybe it's just emotional pain, or maybe it's just an uncomfortable feeling that doesn't even need a name right now.

Many people who are going through divorce are in love with their particular life drama. Their stories are their identities. This leads to thoughts like: *This divorce is killing me; I can't stand it any longer; How long will this hell go on for?* and *I'll never survive this*! that move through their minds constantly.

But none of them are *you*. They're just your mind's understandable reaction when it's not ready to accept the emotional pain and it wants circumstances to be different.

Purposefully let go of the 'selfing' thoughts. Let go of those thoughts that want circumstances to be different, even in the face of incontrovertible evidence that they are the way they are right now.

> Can you accept things just as they are right now, in this very moment, although you hate them?

Step back purposefully from the hatred and the anger and the resentment and the judging, and just accept things as they are right now.

Don't say: 'I am afraid' or 'I am angry' or 'I am unhappy' – which turn 'I' into the fear, the anger, or the unhappiness. Fear or anger or unhappiness has nothing to do with who you are.

It would be more accurate to say, 'I have fearful thoughts' or 'I have angry feelings' or 'There is unhappiness in me.' In this way you emphasize that you're not the content of your thoughts and feelings, and that you don't identify with them.

Instead, you're simply aware of them and you accept them. Now your thoughts cannot drive you relentlessly to even more fear, more anger, and more unhappiness.

Self-Awareness

The ego (the voice in the head) can severely hamper our ability to do anything or even to see situations clearly. We may believe that we know what we're thinking or feeling. But this is an incomplete knowing, at best.

In reality, we're driven by the ego and its limited perspective, totally unaware of the tyranny of our own thoughts and the self-destructive behaviors they often lead to.

> Observe how easily your awareness is carried away from the present moment by your thoughts, no matter where you find yourself, no matter the circumstances.

Notice how often during the day you catch yourself thinking about the past or future. You may be shocked.

All that's required to become free from the ego is to be *self-aware*, because awareness and ego are incompatible.

If you're *aware*, you'll be able to recognize the voice in the head for what it is – an old thought, conditioned by the past. You no longer need to believe in every thought you think. It's an old memory, nothing more.

As we've seen, self-awareness is not the same as thought. Awareness is the intelligence that lies beyond thinking. It stands outside the mind's activity, just observing all that's going on inside the mind.

Awareness is like a vessel that holds our thinking. It helps us to witness and know our thoughts as thoughts, rather than getting caught up in them and confusing them for who we are.

Self-awareness is pure, clean, tranquil, selfless, endless, steadfast, eternal, and independent. It is wise, rather than just knowledgeable. It puts an end to our looking to the outside world for reassurance and affirmation; in awareness we only have to look within.

Self-awareness is the power that is concealed within the present moment. The present is the only time in which to know anything, and the only time in which to observe, to learn, to act, to change, to heal.

> Be the ever-alert guardian of your inner space.
>
> - Eckhart Tolle

Start by taking responsibility for your inner state at any given moment. Ask yourself:

> Is there any negativity in me at this moment?

Then, become attentive to your thoughts and emotions. With awareness you're able to dis-identify from thoughts, emotions, and reactions, which causes them to become de-personalized. There is no longer a sense of self in them. They're simply human thoughts, human emotions, human reactions.

Your sense of self – who you are – undergoes a shift. Before you *were* the thoughts, emotions, and reactions. Now you're the *awareness*, the conscious presence, that witnesses them.

When this shift happens – which is the shift from thinking (ego) to awareness – an intelligence far greater than the ego's cunning begins to operate in your life.

Your life drama – which is no more than a bundle of thoughts and emotions – no longer occupies the forefront of your consciousness. It no longer forms the basis of your identity. You're the present awareness that's prior to and deeper than any thought or emotion.

Awareness doesn't fluctuate at all with your mental state or life circumstances. It knows deeply that whatever is present in this moment – whatever happened to shake up your life and threatens to overwhelm you – will of itself inevitably change. *This, too, shall pass.*

Awareness is not an attempt to escape from difficulties and emotional pain by entering into some 'meditative' state of denial. Awareness doesn't mean rejecting the bad, condemning anything or anybody, or wishing things were different.

On the contrary, being aware is a willingness to go nose-to-nose with emotional pain, confusion, or loss if that is what's dominating the present moment.

Only in aware presence will you find a way to come to terms with, and to move beyond, your unpleasant thoughts and emotions – not through fretful doing, but by watching them, feeling them fully, and letting them be, moment by moment.

The storms of your divorce will still have to run their course; you will have to feel their pain. But these storms actually unfold differently when they're cradled in awareness.

The life situation of divorce, and the emotional pain it causes, are no longer just happening *to* you, like some outside force. In self-awareness, you take responsibility for what you feel, because this is what's happening in your life at this moment.

Relating to your pain consciously – in awareness – as long as it's here anyway, allows you to be a participant with your thoughts and feelings, rather than a victim of them. The more you can be aware of your thoughts and emotions, the less likely you are to be carried away by them.

Awareness takes it all in and serves as a source of peace within the turmoil, much like a parent is a source of peace, compassion, and perspective for a child who's upset.

It's also not that awareness is the answer to all of life's problems. Rather, it's that all of life's problems can be seen more clearly through the lens of a clear mind, through the lens of awareness.

Awareness makes it easier to maintain a sense of equilibrium and a sense of perspective, even in the most trying life circumstances. With awareness comes a feeling of spaciousness, of having more room to move, of having more options, of having the freedom to choose an appropriate and effective response to the stressors of divorce, rather than losing our equilibrium and sense of self as a result of feeling overwhelmed, or being thrown off-balance by a knee-jerk, conditioned reaction.

With inner stillness, you become fully aware of the whole picture. You're able to see all the factors that determine your choices from moment to moment. When you're grounded in moment-to-moment awareness, you're more likely to be creative and to see new solutions to problems. Your response is optimal on all levels, not just mechanically reactive.

By becoming aware, you can actually change a situation before you do anything, because awareness gives you a range of options for acting and influencing what happens next.

As the story goes, someone approached the Buddha and asked him: 'Are you a god?' to which he replied: 'No, I am awake.'

The essence of self-awareness is to wake up from the self-imposed half sleep of the ego in which we are so often immersed. Self-awareness allows us to grow into ourselves in fullness and to live our precious and fleeting lives more wisely.

13

Wholeness
(The Illusion of Separateness)

> It's only in our minds that we are separate from the rest of the world.
> - Gay Luce

As we've seen, we live with a mental image of ourselves – the ego – with which we have a tortured relationship.

When you say 'my life', that is the voice of the ego. The ego separates life itself from who you are. If 'I' and 'life' are two separate concepts, then I am separated from life, and thus also separated from all things and all people.

That's why it's not accurate to speak of 'my life'. I *am* life. I and life are one.

As with almost everything else, it's our thinking mind that's also the culprit here. Through our over-reliance on thinking, reality becomes fragmented.

This 'fragmented reality' seems very real when you're trapped in it. But it's ultimately an illusion, because the universe is an indivisible whole in which all things, all people, and all situations are interconnected. Interconnectedness is a fundamental principle of nature. Nothing exists in isolation.

There are two reasons why we perceive reality as fragmented, and ourselves as isolated. The first is our perception, which reduces reality to what is accessible to us through our senses – what we can see, hear, smell, taste, and touch.

The second, more serious reason is compulsive thinking. It's when we're swept along the incessant stream of our thinking that the universe really disintegrates for us, and we lose the ability to sense the interconnectedness of all things.

Our minds, out of habit or sheer unconsciousness, quickly jump to a particular way of seeing things. That's because our view of ourselves and our circumstances are so readily shaped by the prejudices and beliefs, and the 'likes' and 'dislikes' that we've acquired on our journey through life.

Every thought implies perspective. Perspective, by its very nature, implies limitation. Thus, every thought is limited, which ultimately means that it cannot be absolutely true.

This is how the ego tries to stay in charge. It convinces us that we're separate, that we're flawed and broken and alone, instead of what we actually are – *whole*. Don't listen to it.

Our overwhelming preoccupation with our ego-created separate lives ignores another, more fundamental, level of reality.

Einstein reminds us that when we neglect the perspective of wholeness and interconnectedness, we only see one side of being alive. With this view, we inflate the sense of *my* life, *my* problems, *my* loss, *my* pain to become of supreme importance in our lives. When we identify with the ego-created 'self', it's a delusion, a form of self-imprisonment. It prevents us from seeing the very real dimension of our being that is not separate at all.

During her time in India, every time she became aware of the ego trying to encroach on her sense of wholeness, Elizabeth Gilbert repeated the mantra: 'Ham-sa.' This is a Sanskrit word that means: 'I am That; I am an expression of God; I am not separate; I am not alone.'

Our thinking minds are almost always severely fragmented. This is simply the nature of thought. The only way to overcome this fragmentation is through practicing mindfulness.

Awareness, intentionally perceived in every moment, can help us to realize that even in the midst of our mental fragmentation, our fundamental nature remains integrated and whole.

As we've seen, awareness is the pot that cradles the thinking mind, just as a soup pot holds all the individual ingredients of the soup – the carrots, the onions, the celery – allowing them to cook into one whole. Just let all the 'fragments' stir while you hold them in awareness. Whatever comes up in your mind goes into the pot, becomes part of the soup.

Awareness drives home to us the futility of allowing our thinking minds to turn any situation or thing into an absolute, separate existence.

In this way, awareness of interconnectedness might also enhance our appreciation of the impermanence of all things and circumstances and relationships. We might appreciate life more, people more, moments more, if by looking deeply into them, we sense that everything that we're connected to in turn connects us to everything else, and that these connections are only temporary.

As John Steinbeck and Edward Ricketts recorded in *Sea of Cortez*, this awareness:

> [I]s really the understanding and the attempt to say that man is related to the whole thing, related inextricably to all reality, known and

> unknowable…. that all things are one thing and that one thing is all things.

All of life is beautiful and fascinating when the veil of our compulsive thinking lifts, even for a moment.

Wholeness and interconnectedness are the most fundamental components of our nature as living beings. No matter how many scars – emotional and even physical – we carry around from what we've suffered in the past, our intrinsic wholeness is intact.

We neither have to be helpless victims of what someone has done to us in the past or what someone has not done for us in the past, nor do we have to stand helpless in the face of what we're suffering right now.

That's because we are so much more than our scars. We are what was present before the scars – our original wholeness.

Through practicing mindfulness, we can reconnect with our intrinsic wholeness, because it's always present. We can heal the wounds of disconnectedness and the painful feelings of isolation, fragmentation, and separation, if we mindfully reconnect with the underlying wholeness and interconnectedness *within* ourselves.

This means that it's always possible to transcend fragmentation, vulnerability, insecurity, fear, and despair – if we become aware, if we see differently, if we see with eyes of wholeness.

Seeing with eyes of wholeness is healing. It helps us to acknowledge the ways in which we're extraordinary and miraculous, without losing sight of the ways in which we're simultaneously just part of the unfolding larger whole, like waves on the ocean rising and falling back in the brief moments of our lives.

The perspective of wholeness and interconnectedness implies a new and profound coming to terms with our problems and our suffering, and it creates an entirely different context within which we can see our emotional pain and suffering.

Moments in which we experience wholeness and connect with the domain of being often include a palpable sense of being larger than our emotional pain and our problems, and of being in a much better position to come to terms with them.

It's a perceptual shift away from fragmentation and isolation, a shift from feeling helpless, pessimistic, and out of control, to a sense of the possible, a sense of acceptance and inner peace and control.

In other words, the more conscious we can become of the interconnectedness of our thoughts and feelings and choices and actions in the world, the more we can see with eyes of wholeness, and the more effective we can be when faced with resentment, alienation, obstacles, challenges, and the stress of divorce.

Feeling whole, even for brief periods, nourishes us on a deep level. It's a source of wisdom and healing in the face of the emotional pain of divorce.

> You have transcended the separation that thought creates.
> You are the present moment in all its fullness.
>
> - Anonymous

14

Non-Doing (Being) and Stillness (Space)

Many people going through divorce tend to feel completely caught up in the demands of their job, supporting a family, their financial situation, or simply the mundane routines of daily living that seem to deprive their lives of significance.

Many are consumed by acute stress, anxiety, depression, anger, and loneliness. Many yearn for the freedom that they believe financial security promises, while others, who already enjoy financial security, know that it's not enough to endow their lives with meaning.

Our lives have both an inner and outer purpose. Our inner purpose concerns what we *are* and is primary. Our outer purpose is about what we *do* and is secondary.

This simply means that our primary purpose is not our goals, desires, intentions, and the actions that we take to achieve them, but rather the state of awareness out of which they come.

Simply put, being is primary; doing is secondary.

Non-Doing

It's important not to confuse *non-doing* with doing nothing. They could not be more different. Non-doing has nothing to do with being passive. What matters in non-doing is our state of awareness.

The demands and stressors of divorce leave us scant time for non-doing unless we seize it on purpose. The effort is worthwhile. Moments of non-doing are one of the greatest gifts you can give yourself.

In non-doing, you consciously shift from 'doing' mode into 'being' mode. You let go of all your doing and you purposefully allow your mind to come to rest in the present moment, no matter what's 'on' your mind.

Simply allow yourself to be in the moment with things exactly as they are, without trying to change anything. In other words, you practice 'being'.

To practice non-doing (being), you don't have to stop all doing and isolate yourself in a room in complete silence. As we've said before, the idea is to create a little island of non-doing in the sea of constant doing, a time for all 'doing' to stop.

You can do this anywhere and at any time – sitting in traffic, waiting outside the school to pick up your children, sitting in your lawyer's waiting room, standing in line at the supermarket, leaving your cubicle to stretch your legs and get a drink of water, waiting for the train, cooking dinner, or walking the dog.

In these moments, instead of instinctively reaching for your phone, just tune into the present moment and be *aware* from one moment to the next. A few seconds of 'non-doing' many times throughout the day are all you need.

As we've said all along, mindfulness involves being aware of whatever the present moment presents – if you're tense, be aware of the tension; if you're angry, then be with the anger as best you can; if you're beating yourself up about something you said to your partner, then observe the activity of your judging mind.

The benefits of non-doing are twofold. First, you come to see that nothing else needs to happen in *this* moment to make it complete. This moment – whatever form it takes – arrived complete.

Second, you realize that the only way in which you can do anything worthwhile is to have the effort (doing) come out of non-doing (being). Otherwise, self-involvement, greed, or struggle can sneak in and poison your relationship with the 'doing', thereby draining all the joy from the endeavor, and leaving you dissatisfied.

> Sitting quietly in non-doing, Spring comes and the grass grows all by itself.
> - Zenrin

Stillness

> Stillness is the language God speaks.
> Everything else is a bad translation.
>
> - Anonymous

We've already talked about how important it is to set aside some quiet time every day. Quiet time is a vital part of life, and a quiet mind is the foundation for inner peace. Peace can only exist in a quiet mind.

> Silence without,
> stillness within.
>
> - Anonymous

But quiet time is not the same as the 'stillness' we're talking about here, although quiet time is one of the best gateways to that 'stillness'.

The concept of 'stillness' relates to the image of the lake we've encountered before. The outer situation of your life, your external circumstances, is the surface of the lake. Sometimes it's calm, other times it's windy and choppy, according to the seasons. Deep down, however, the lake is always undisturbed.

You are the whole lake, not just the surface. To be 'still' is to be in touch with your own depth, which always remains absolutely undisturbed.

Practicing mindfulness is about connecting with the stillness and peace at the core of your being, deep beneath the surface agitations of your mind. It's as simple as seeing a thought and letting it go, seeing an emotion and letting it go – all the while using your breath as an anchor to remind yourself to stay focused and calm.

'Stillness' is synonymous with 'space'. Every time you become aware of the present moment – even if you only catch a glimpse of it – you briefly step out of the voice in your head (your thought process) and its reflection in your body as emotion.

Non-Doing (Being) and Stillness (Space)

Inner spaciousness arises where before there was only the clutter of thought and the turmoil of emotion. Inner spaciousness comes as stillness – a subtle peace deep within you, even in the face of something seemingly upsetting.

You realize that *this, too, shall pass*. Suddenly there's space around the 'upsetting' event. There's space around your emotional pain. From that space emanates a peace that is not of this world, a peace that 'passeth all understanding'. This is the peace of God.

You're never more essentially, more deeply, yourself than when you're still. After all, you cannot see your own reflection in running water.

In moments of stillness, you come to realize that you are already whole, already complete in your being. You have a sense of self-acceptance, of spaciousness. You come to realize the fullness of *this* moment, of *this* breath, and you find peace.

Dwelling in mindful stillness is one of the most meaningful things you can possibly do – coming to peace with your own mind, reconnecting with yourself.

The more you're able to incorporate 'stillness' in your daily life, the greater your perspective becomes to view events as 'small stuff', rather than emergencies, and, therefore, the less reactive and irritable you will be.

> It is not to be learned by running away from things, turning solitary and going apart from the world. Rather, one must learn inner solitude, wherever and with whomever he may be.
>
> - Father Eckhart

The moment you become rooted in mindful stillness, space arises. This space manifests as the gap between each thought and emotion that you have, and your response thereto. For example, in the still space after your partner makes a snide comment, you observe the way in which you would usually react, and you consciously choose a different response.

From spacious awareness comes depth, equanimity, compassion, and wisdom. Your view of life becomes open, clear, and detached. You have a lightness, an ease in daily living, an ability to keep perspective, and even a sense of humor about your predicaments.

> Only in this silence – the silence underneath thought – can one hear the symphony of the universe, can one hear the whisper of God, can one approach the inner temple wherein dwells the soul.
>
> - Anonymous

15

Fear and Anxiety

> Courage is not the towering oak that sees the storms come and go; it is the fragile blossom that opens in the snow.
>
> - Alice Swaim

Fear

The underlying emotion that governs all activity of the ego is *fear* – the fear that bad things will happen, the fear that good things won't last, the fear that other people might hurt us, the fear of being nobody, the fear of non-existence, the fear of death.

The ego is sustained by what Deepak Chopra calls *'object referral'*. In object-referral, our internal reference point is not our self-awareness but, rather, we're influenced by 'objects' outside ourselves – situations, circumstances, people, and things.

In object referral we constantly seek the approval of others; our thinking and behavior are always in anticipation of a response; we have an intense need to control things; we crave external power. The need for approval, the need to control things, and the need for external power are all based in fear.

Painful family relationships, often strained to breaking point by divorce, cause us fear and worry and can make us feel helpless, hopeless, and defeated.

We've all seen, heard about, read about, or experienced for ourselves, divorces that contain a churning, ugly energy like a tornado. The desire to hurt our partners is, ultimately, also born out of fear.

Overcoming the desire to hurt our partners requires that we see our own fears, that we understand them, and that we own them. Owning our fears means taking responsibility for them; taking responsibility for them means not letting fear completely dictate our views and experiences of divorce.

If we interpret an event as 'threatening', then it will induce fear in us. Fearful, frantic thinking takes an enormous amount of energy and drains the creativity and motivation from our lives.

But if we view the 'threatening' event in a different light, perhaps as an opportunity, then the same event might not cause us any fear, or at least a good deal less fear.

It can be particularly helpful to keep in mind, from moment to moment, that it's not so much the fear that we experience, but how we see it and what we do with it, that determines the extent to which we're at its mercy. If we change the way we see, we can change the way in which we respond.

It's not that we must try to become free of fear. The moment we try to free ourselves from fear, we create resistance against the fear. Resistance, in any form, cannot end fear.

Rather than trying to run away or control or suppress fearful feelings, we need to come directly into contact with them, to learn about them, and to understand them.

> Fear is a question.
> What are you afraid of and why?
> Our fears are a treasure house of self-knowledge if we explore them.
>
> - Marilyn Ferguson

The way of mindfulness is to accept ourselves right now as we are – fear or no fear. Instead of rejecting our experiences as undesirable, we allow ourselves, for this moment at least, to go right into the full-blown feeling.

> Feel the fear and do it anyway.
>
> - Susan Jeffers

Facing your fear requires some courage. But you can at least 'dip your toe' in, trying just a little – say for one breath – to move in for a closer look. As you do this, maybe you'll discover that fear itself is not something 'to fear' – it's just a feeling. It may be unpleasant, but it can't kill you.

> As closely as you dare, look at your fear and at your feelings about your fear, and accept them just as they are.

It's important to face your fear, because frightening thoughts or experiences can easily lead to a state of panic, desperation, and a feeling of complete loss of control. To panic is a very dangerous reaction because it's disabling exactly at the time that you most need to keep your wits about you and you most need to solve problems with clarity.

Anxiety

If we're honest with ourselves, most of us would have to admit that we live our lives in an ocean of fear. This sad state of affairs is evident in the habitual maladaptive patterns that we develop, such as passivity or aggressiveness to compensate for our insecurities, and in our becoming overwhelmed and incapacitated by the very feeling of fear when it surfaces.

Anxiety is also a strongly reactive emotional state similar to fear, but without a clearly identifiable threat. It's a generalized state of insecurity and agitation that can be triggered by almost anything.

In divorce, we're often plagued by anxious feelings that frequently seem out of proportion to the actual pressures that we experience. We may find ourselves worrying all the time, even when there's no immediate threat. We always seem to *find something* to worry about.

Many people also experience anxiety attacks or panic attacks – discrete periods of intense fear and discomfort for no apparent reason. The first time you suffer a panic attack, you may think that you're having a heart attack, because it frequently manifests in physical symptoms such as chest pains, shortness of breath, dizziness, and profuse sweating.

We can work with these mind-body storms by changing the way in which we pay attention to the thoughts and reactivity within our own minds.

The mindfulness instructions emphasize that we don't have to *do* anything about bodily sensations or anxious feelings, except to become aware of them and to stop judging them and condemning ourselves.

In mindful awareness we realize that we are not our anxiety and fears, and that they don't have to rule our lives.

Mindfulness teaches us to go 'underneath' the surface agitations of our minds into a state of deeper calmness. As we've seen, the image of the lake teaches us that it's possible to trust a stable inner core within ourselves that's reliable, dependable, and unwavering.

While the surface of our minds may be agitated and 'choppy' – like the surface of the lake – we can learn to accept that this is simply the way that the mind is at times, while at the same time experiencing an underlying inner peace.

Gradually the sense of worry and anxiety in our minds and the tension in our bodies become less acute and lose some of their force.

We have to learn to not give up on ourselves. We have to be willing to face our lives in all their richness – in both pleasant and unpleasant circumstances, when things are going the way that we want and when they're not, when we feel that things are under control and when we don't – and to use these experiences and our own thoughts and feelings as the raw materials for healing ourselves.

> Courage takes many forms.
> There is physical courage, there is moral courage.
> Then there is a still higher type of courage – the courage to brave pain, to live with it, and to still find joy in life; to wake up in the morning with enthusiasm for the day ahead.
>
> - Howard Cossell

16

Victimhood and Anger

The deeply conditioned habits of our mind and the emotional scars we carry, can cause toxic consequences in our lives. They often leave us feeling desperately inadequate about facing and surviving the life circumstance of divorce.

Two of the most toxic consequences that our lives can exhibit in the midst of divorce are victimhood and anger.

Victimhood

As we've seen, people are in love with their own life dramas. Their stories become their identity.

Don't let your mind use your pain to create a *victim identity* for yourself. A victim identity is the belief that other people and what they did to you in the past are responsible for who you are now. Feeling sorry for yourself and burdening others with your story will keep you stuck in suffering.

As long as you're the victim of other people's behavior, you live as if you're not responsible, as if you're not able to choose your response to your partner's behavior. To paraphrase Stephen Covey, victimhood is present when your internal dialogue goes something like this:

'If only things were different. But it's just the way things are.' (In other words: *There is nothing I can do.*)

'If only he didn't do that. He makes me so angry!' (In other words: *Something outside of my control determines my emotional life.*)

'If only I did this when I was younger. I can't look for a job now. I don't have the time.' (In other words: *Something outside me – a lack of time – controls me.*)

'If only I had a different judge, one who was more undestanding.' (In other words: *Someone else's behavior is limiting my effectiveness.*)

On a deeply unconscious level, we don't want to let go of our victim identities. Victimhood can become seductively easy and familiar. Self-pity comes so naturally to all of us. We don't want positive change because that would threaten our identities as disheartened or oppressed people.

And if friends or family no longer want to listen to our sad stories, we can keep telling them to ourselves in our heads over and over and feel sorry for ourselves. In this way we can hold on to our identities as victims who were done in by our partners, life, the universe, or God.

But instead of admitting that they won't do anything about their victim identities, some people say: 'I can't'. But deep down we know that 'I can't' is a lie. It's just an irresponsible way of saying: 'I won't'.

To feel sorry for yourself is one of the most disintegrating things that you can do to yourself. Elizabeth Elliot, who was widowed twice before the age of forty-eight, said:

> Self-pity is a death that has no resurrection, a sinkhole from which no rescuing hand can drag you because you have chosen to sink.

Self-pity is a bar to progress, and it cuts you off from effective communication with your loved ones because of its inordinate demands for attention and sympathy. It is one of the most dangerous forms of self-centeredness. It fogs your vision.

It's only when we're mindful that we really observe our inner dialogue with any detachment and ponder its validity, especially as far as it concerns our thoughts and beliefs about ourselves.

Victimhood and Anger

For example, if you're in the habit of saying to yourself, 'I could never do that', when you encounter a problem in your divorce that requires you to speak up for yourself or do something for the first time, one thing is certain – you won't be able to. At that moment your thought makes real its own content. Saying 'I can't' becomes a self-fulfilling prophesy.

By the time that you have a chance to act or to do something to solve the problem, you've already enclosed yourself in a box of your own creation and you've limited the possibilities open to you. If your thoughts, feelings, and beliefs always produce reasons for not rising to a challenge, for not taking a risk, for not exploring what might be possible for you, then you might be unnecessarily limiting your own growth and your ability to make changes in your life.

When we're mindful of the process of thought itself, we can more easily catch our own lapses of mind, our faulty thinking, and the self-defeating behaviors that often result.

To a great extent, our ability to influence our life circumstances depends on how we see things. How we see things sometimes affects how much energy we have for doing certain things, and it affects our choices about where to channel the energy we do have.

The truth is that we really don't know what we're capable of in any particular situation. Our beliefs about ourselves and our own capabilities sometimes affect what we find possible.

So, be open to your potential to exercise control over the specific events in your life; be open to your potential to make things happen, even when you might have to face new, unpredictable, or stressful life circumstances.

Anger

Many people going through divorce are consumed with anger, bitterness, and self-justification towards their partners. In a negative sense, psychologically speaking, they're still married. Each needs the weakness of the other to justify his/her accusations.

Hard as it is for us to admit, especially about ourselves, self-tinged anger is something we indulge in, and surrender to, far too often.

But anger is, without a doubt, one of the most toxic reactions you can have towards your partner or some other person or situation in your divorce drama. The anger festers inside of you, calling for your attention.

> You will not be punished for your anger. You will be punished by your anger.
>
> - Buddha

Victimhood and Anger

I always come away from an angry encounter feeling that there's something inadequate about anger, even when, objectively, I had the moral high ground. Its innate toxicity, and the self-absorption and self-righteousness that often accompany it, taint all they touch.

When we get angry our hands tend to close into fists. The next time you find yourself making fists out of anger, try to bring self-awareness to the inner attitude symbolized by the fist. Can you feel the tension, the aggression, and the fear which the fist contains?

Anger is a powerful – but also utterly useless – reaction to your partner and the life situation of divorce. Think back: *What good has ever come out of any situation to which you added the burden of your anger?* When has reacting with anger ever brought you good results? After you'd reacted in anger, how many times did you regret it and wished that your partner did not have the power to push your buttons?

> He who angers you, conquers you.
>
> - Elizabeth Kenny

I have seen clients who are slowly being crushed by the burden of their anger. Their anger is poisoning them.

> Anger is an acid that can do more harm to the vessel in which it is stored than to anything on which it is poured.

- Mark Twain

Through self-awareness you can create *space* between the match (the external stimulus – your partner, your child, your lawyer, the judge, the court system, or the universe) and your 'involuntary' flare-up (your angry reaction).

As we've seen, the most effective way to become self-aware is to become aware of your breathing. Especially during those moments when you feel anger boil up inside of you, focusing on your breath takes attention away from thinking and creates space.

When you get angry, your breathing gets shallow and quick. Under these circumstances, just one conscious breath is enough to make space where before there was the uninterrupted succession of one angry thought after the other.

In that space created by self-awareness you see the way in which you would usually react, but now you have the power to choose your response. And when you consciously choose your response, it will most likely not be anger, because in awareness you know that anger is negative, destructive, and that it will only put you under another person's power.

The point is not to deny or repress your anger, but through self-awareness to acknowledge that it's there, to gain insight into where it came from, to realize that your awareness is bigger than the anger, and then to consciously set the anger aside and choose a different, productive response.

17

Unhappiness

> Man in unhappy because he doesn't know that he's happy. If anyone finds out he'll become happy at once.
>
> - Fyodor Dostoyevsky

I once met with a client towards the end of his long, acrimonious divorce. He said to me: 'I'm so glad that this is almost over. My life has become unbearable. I can't take any more pain.' After a pensive pause he continued: 'I guess what I'm saying is that I'm just fed up with being unhappy.'

Eckhart Tolle describes unhappiness as 'an ego-created emotional disease that has reached epidemic proportions in modern society.' It's the inner equivalent of the environmental pollution of our planet.

We don't even recognize negative emotional states such as anxiety, anger, resentment, discontent, and jealousy as negative anymore. We not only believe that they're totally justified, but also that some other person or external factor caused them. In other words, we don't believe that they're self-created. The ego screams incessantly: 'I hold [you] [what you've done to me] [what's happened to me] responsible for my pain!'

Of course, the ego cannot distinguish between an actual situation and its interpretation of and rection to the situation. The ego might prompt you to say, 'What awful weather!' without you realizing that the wind or sleet or rain is not 'awful'. It just is. It is as it is. What's 'awful' is the ego's interpretation of and reaction to the weather, and consequently your resistance to it and the emotion that your resistance creates.

I have a friend in New York who belongs to a running club. The runners take pride in the fact that there are almost no weather conditions that prevent them from taking to the road. Many a time during a Northeastern winter I would say to my friend: 'I can't believe you went out in this weather!' Her response has always been the same: 'There's no such thing as bad weather. There's only inadequate clothing.'

> There is nothing either good or bad, but thinking makes it so.
>
> - William Shakespeare

The primary cause of unhappiness is never a particular situation, but our thoughts about the situation.

Be aware of the thoughts you think. Separate your thoughts about a situation from the actual situation. Your awareness looks at the situation and says to your mind: *'There is the situation. Here are my thoughts about the situation.'* As we've seen, your awareness serves as the vessel in which negative mental-emotional states are contained and transmuted.

For example, 'My partner ruined my life', is a story. Stories limit you and prevent you from taking effective action. 'My partner filed for divorce', is a fact. Facing facts is empowering.

Remember that what you think by and large creates the emotions that you feel. Be aware of the link between your thoughts and emotions.

The next time you feel angry or sad, direct your attention inside and see if you can sense the emotion directly, instead of through the filter of your unhappy thoughts. At this moment, anger or sadness is what you feel. There's nothing you can do about the fact that *at this moment* you feel angry or sad. Instead of wanting this moment to be different – which just adds more emotional pain to the pain you already experience – ask yourself:

> Is it possible to completely accept that this is how I feel at this moment?
> Can I allow these feelings to simply be there?

The moment you stop identifying with the feeling of anger or sadness, the moment you put your attention directly on it without trying to resist it, the feeling can no longer control your thinking.

Infinite possibilities open up when you become aware – other, vastly more intelligent ways of dealing with any life circumstance. Unhappiness can never be intelligent because it's always from the ego.

Whenever you feel negativity arising within you – whether caused by an external circumstance, a thought, an emotion, or even nothing in particular that you can identify – look at it in awareness and say to yourself:

> Attention!
> Get out of your mind!
> Be here now!

As Eckhart Tolle reminds us: 'When you recognize that the present moment is always already the case – that it is inevitable – you can bring an uncompromising inner "yes" to it.' In this way you don't create further unhappiness for yourself.

What's more, with inner resistance gone you become empowered. Now you can examine what steps you can take, given your unhappiness right now, that would help you to move towards greater peace and harmony in your life.

Each negative event either opens our eyes to an opportunity to change the course of our lives for the better, or sends us down a bottomless pit of pain, suffering, and self-abuse.

We are not fated to live the rest of our lives in emotional turmoil and unhappiness. We are not bound to decisions that we made or that were made for us years ago, perhaps when we were young and insecure.

In divorce, our unhappiness is almost always out of proportion to the apparent cause. We overreact. We easily find reasons for being upset, angry, fearful, or despondent.

Some comment or action by our partners, that someone else would shrug off without giving it a second thought, becomes the apparent source for intense unhappiness. We interpret the triggering comment or action through the perspective of a deeply emotional ego, which completely distorts the significance of the trigger.

Our partners' comment or action is not the real cause of our unhappiness; it's simply the trigger that brings out the unhappiness that's been hiding within us all along in the form of old, accumulated emotions. These emotions then move into our minds and set off the ego in a torrent of thinking.

We're trapped in our own ego-created hell.

Like my client, many people reach a point where they feel that they cannot live with their unhappy selves anymore. Inner peace then becomes their greatest priority. Their acute emotional pain forces them to dis-identify with the content of their minds that perpetuate the story of 'poor, unhappy me'. They finally realize that neither their unhappy stories nor the unhappy emotions that they experience are who they truly are.

Sadly, when we try to seek happiness, we end up postponing it, often indefinitely. We don't consciously set out to do so, but we keep convincing ourselves that: *'When I'm free from my partner, I'll be happy', 'My life will be complete when…'*

Meanwhile, life keeps marching forward. In truth, there's no better time to be happy than right now. If not now, when?

> For a long time, it seemed to me that
> life was about to begin.
> But there was always some obstacle in the
> way, something to be got through first,
> some unfinished business…. Then life
> would begin.
> At last, it dawned on me that these
> obstacles were my life.
>
> - Alfred D'Souza

Your life will always be filled with challenges and uncertainty. It's best to admit this to yourself and decide to be happy anyway.

> There is no way to happiness.
> Happiness is the way.
>
> - Anonymous

18

Patience

> Adopt the pace of nature: her secret is patience.
>
> - Ralph Waldo Emerson

In modern society, the things that we have to wait for are getting fewer and fewer. We don't have to wait for the newspaper to get the news in the morning; we can just open the news feeds on our phones. We don't have to wait for a movie to start at the local theatre; we can simply stream it. We don't have to wait for an opportunity to get to a store to buy something; we can simply order it online to arrive on our doorstep the next morning.

Our opportunities to practice patience are becoming fewer and fewer. Unfortunately, divorce is one of those life circumstances that can test our patience to the utmost. You've probably found yourself thinking something like: *Yes, I know this divorce, too, will pass! But when!*

In their initial consultation with me, clients would inevitably ask me how long I thought their divorce would take. My answer was always the same: 'Unfortunately, anything that someone wants to make an issue in divorce becomes an issue. The divorce will only proceed as quickly as the slowest person is willing to allow it to go, and it will only be as easy as the most difficult person is willing to allow it to be.' I'm sure that this, too, has been your experience.

The Seasons Cannot be Hurried

The truth is that everything – including divorce – unfolds in its own time. The seasons cannot be hurried. When Spring comes, the grass grows; not before.

Being in a hurry rarely helps. On the contrary, impatience can create a great deal of suffering for you and for those around you.

Scratch the surface of impatience and you'll find that anger – subtly or even not so subtly – lurks just beneath the surface. It's the strong negative energy of not wanting things to be as they are and of blaming someone – yourself or others – for the way that things are.

When we realize that things unfold according to their own nature, we can come to accept that our life's journey unfolds in the same way. We don't have to let our anxieties and our desire for a certain result dominate the quality of the present moment – even when things are painful (as they so often are in divorce).

Patience doesn't mean that we can never hurry when we have to. It's possible to hurry patiently and mindfully because we've chosen to do so.

Patience is the alternative to the mind's endemic restlessness. With mindfulness we attempt to bring balance into the present moment. We know that in patience lies wisdom, and that what will come next is determined in large measure by our state of consciousness in this moment.

By cultivating patience, we're tilling the soil of our own minds to ensure that they can serve as a source of clarity, compassion, and right action in any life circumstance.

> Do you have the patience to wait until your mud settles and the water is clear again?
> Can you remain unmoving until the right action arises by itself?
>
> - Lao-Tzu

At times, when you feel under pressure and obstructed in something that you want or need to do, it can be especially useful to look attentively in awareness at the impatience and anger that inevitably arise.

See if you can adopt a different perspective, one that sees things unfolding in their own time. Hard as it may be, try not to push the river along in that moment, but listen carefully to it instead.

As you attend the gentle flow of your breath while you practice mindfulness, notice the pull of your mind to get on to something else, to want to change what's happening – that's impatience.

Instead of losing yourself in your thoughts, try to sit patiently with your breath and with keen awareness of what's unfolding in each moment, allowing it to unfold as it will without imposing anything on it. Just watch and breathe, while embodying stillness and becoming patient.

Mindfulness must be kindled and nurtured, protected from the gusts of wind of a busy life and from a restless and tormented mind, just as a small flame needs to be sheltered. In return, mindfulness will reward you with peace and patience.

Be Patient with Yourself

Just like forgiveness, we cannot be patient with other people before we've learned to be patient with ourselves.

Intentionally remind yourself not to get impatient with yourself just because you find your mind judging all the time, or because you're tense, agitated, or fearful.

Give yourself room to have these experiences. Why? Because they're here anyway; you're experiencing them anyway! When impatience or anger or resentment or loneliness rears its ugly head, it's your reality in that moment; it's part of life unfolding in that moment. Don't rush through these moments just because they're unpleasant. After all, each one *is your life* in that moment.

As you've no doubt experienced during even a few minutes of practicing mindfulness, your mind has a 'mind of its own'. One of your mind's favorite activities is to lose itself in thinking and to wander into the past and into the future.

Much of the time our thoughts overwhelm our awareness of the present moment and cause us to lose our connection to the present moment. Patiently accept this wandering tendency of your mind while reminding yourself that you don't have to get caught up in its travels.

Cultivating Patience

Without patience, life is extremely frustrating. You easily get annoyed, bothered, and irritated.

The more patient you are, the more accepting you will be of *what is*, rather than insisting that life be different from what it is now or that life be exactly as you'd like it to be now.

Patience adds a dimension of ease and acceptance to your life that's essential for inner peace.

Cultivating patience means opening yourself to the present moment, even if it's unpleasant or painful. If you're late for an appointment with your lawyer because you're stuck in traffic, opening to the present moment means catching yourself building a mental snowball before your thinking gets completely out of control, and gently reminding yourself to relax.

If you remain aware enough, you can almost always see the innocence in 'frustrating' circumstances and 'annoying' people. If you can do this, you'll become a more patient and peaceful person. In some strange way, you actually begin to enjoy the challenge of remaining mindful in moments that would have been frustrating to you before.

Being patient allows you to keep perspective. You can remember, even in the midst of the most trying circumstances, that the challenge in this moment is not 'life or death', but just a minor obstacle that has to be dealt with.

In the confrontation between the stream and the rock, the stream always wins… not through strength, but through patience.

- Anonymous

19

Forgiveness

> It is in pardoning that we are pardoned.
>
> - St. Francis of Assisi

I agonized about whether to include some thoughts on forgiveness in this book. That's because I know that some readers are at that stage of the dissolution of their marriages where forgiveness is unthinkable. The last thing that they want to hear is that they should forgive their partners.

I'm not asking you to do anything that you don't yet feel ready to even consider. I'd just like to share some thoughts with you for a time when you might feel more open to the idea of forgiveness. Like all feelings and life circumstances, this aversion you feel to the very idea of forgiveness, too, shall pass.

The Villain in Our Stories

Failed relationships leave behind a powerful residue of pain, sadness, distrust, and doubt.

Our partners often become the scapegoats for our suffering because they can't win no matter what they do. The odds were stacked against them from the very beginning.

Many people look to have all of their emotional, physical, financial, and spiritual needs met by that 'one special person', a savior who'll take away all of their isolation, sadness, and pain.

And then, of course, that 'special person' we thought we married, turns out to be…well…just a person. Our dreams get washed away in a tide of disappointment. We become angry, bitter, and resentful.

If we're willing to believe that someone else is our savior and the source of all our happiness, chances are that we're going to be equally willing to believe that the same someone is the cause of all our suffering.

In divorce, it's so tempting to pin the blame for all our suffering on our partners. Our default setting seems to be: *When in doubt, it must be my partner's fault.* Every story needs a villain, and in the story of 'unhappy me', our partners make the perfect villains. We believe – wrongly – that when we make our partners the villains, we'll feel better about ourselves.

Of course, making our partners the villains in our stories doesn't make us feel better. In fact, it has the exact opposite effect. When we're in the habit of blaming other people for our anger, frustration, depression, stress, and unhappiness, it only leads to more anger, more sadness, more bitterness, more distrust, and more damage. It points us down a dark road. We cannot be at peace.

If you think about it, in its essence, divorce is a process of letting go. A client once told me: 'You know, I've come to realize that divorce is an adventure in forgiveness.'

Forgive to Take Back Control

It helped me tremendously when I realized that forgiveness is not an act that you do for someone else, but that it is largely something that you do to help yourself.

If you can't forgive, *you* are the one who has to carry the burden of your resentment and other negative feelings. Blaming other people takes an enormous amount of mental energy. It's a 'drag-me-down' mindset that creates stress and disease.

Blaming others leaves you feeling powerless over your own life, because your happiness is contingent upon the actions and behaviors of others – which you cannot control.

When you forgive, you regain your sense of personal power. You see yourself as a choice maker. You know that when you experience a negative feeling, *you* play the major part in creating that feeling. This means that *you* can also play the major part in creating new, more positive feelings.

Forgiveness doesn't mean your partner escapes accountability; it means that you hold yourself accountable for your own happiness and for your own reactions to other people and for your own life circumstances. Life is a great deal more fun and easier to manage when you forgive people.

Forgiveness isn't even something that you have to do out loud. It is, above all, a deep transformation withing your own heart.

Forgiving Yourself

I used to struggle a lot with forgiving people. Then it dawned on me that I couldn't even think of forgiving other people before I forgave myself.

There will be many times when you lose it with your partner or your kids, when you unconsciously fall back into being uptight, frustrated, stressed, and reactive. That's okay. Life is a process. When you lose it, just start again!

> I learned that true forgiveness includes total self-acceptance. And out of acceptance wounds are healed and happiness is possible again.
>
> - Catharine Marshall

When you can learn to keep perspective and to stay loving toward yourself, you'll be well on your way to be more loving towards others.

Compassion

Forgiveness doesn't mean to excuse any wrongs your partner has done, to allow him/her to evade responsibility, or to indulge him/her engaging in harmful actions towards you or your loved ones. It means to increase the spacious feeling of understanding and compassion, to take some of the heat off your partner, and to take a more compassionate view of your partner. As the Talmud teaches us:

> When man has compassion for others, God has compassion for him.

When you become aware of feelings of anger or resentment towards your partner, try to look at the situation through your partner's eyes. Perhaps you'll find that your partner is behaving just like you would if you were in his/her shoes.

As Gabriel Cohen reminds us: 'Maybe they're not the storybook villain you've built them up to be in your mind, maybe they're just a person like you: scared like you, selfish like you, mean and kind and intolerant and generous and unforgiving and angry and capable of love, just like you.' You come to see your partner as a suffering being – just like you.

> Forgiveness is the act of admitting that we are like other people.
>
> - Christina Baldwin

Why waste time getting angry at someone who wrongs us? They're only being propelled by their delusions in the same way we are. We're reminded of Yeats's line: 'Why, what could she have done, being what she is?'

> He that cannot forgive others
> breaks a bridge over which
> he must pass himself;
> for every man has need
> to be forgiven.
>
> - Thomas Fuller

You want to get to a place in your own being where you can intentionally cultivate feelings of kindness, generosity, and compassion towards your partner; where you can let go of your feelings of resentment and dislike of your partner; where you can remind yourself to see your partner as a whole being, as someone who deserves love and kindness – just like you, as someone who feels pain and anxiety – just like you, as someone who suffers – just like you.

You purposefully forgive your partner for the hurt that he/she has caused you, dropping the anger and resentment and bitterness that you've been clinging to for dear life, and letting go of your feelings of righteousness.

This leads to a strong release of pent-up negative emotions. It's a profound process of coming to terms in your own heart and mind with the way things are at the moment, a deep letting go of past feelings and hurt.

If you clear out from your mind all the grudges and grievances you obsess over incessantly, you'll discover that you have some space where before there was only clutter. Then God can use that space as a doorway to rush in and fill you with love, and you, too, will be able to say:

> Today, I forgive all those who have offended me. I give my love to all thirsty hearts, both to those who love me and to those who do not love me.
>
> - Anonymous

20

The Journey Ahead

Savor the Moment

> You gain strength, courage, and confidence by every experience
> in which you really stop to look fear in the face.
> You are able to say to yourself,
> 'I lived through this horror.
> I can take the next thing that comes along.'
>
> - Eleanor Roosevelt

Divorce is not a gift that I would have chosen, and it's definitely not one that I would be pleased to receive again. There's no way around it: Divorce sucks!

However, while practicing mindfulness one day soon after my own divorce, I was flooded by an overwhelming sense of relief. Something I had feared greatly had actually happened, and I discovered that I could survive it. There was a lightness, a profound sense of freedom that came from discovering that I could go through a traumatic life experience and come out on the other side. That gave me some confidence that I'll be able to face other big challenges.

The fact is that you've come through one of the most brutal life circumstances that anyone can experience. You've come through the 'dark night of the soul'. You might be battered and bruised – physically, emotionally, and financially – but you're still standing.

Take time to savor the moment, and to appreciate how far you've come.

I want to end our journey together with some practical advice and lessons that I've learned, both from my clients and my own experience, for the road after divorce.

Your New Relationship

Few people are so scarred by divorce that they never want to be in a relationship again. Marriage is the most intimate, the most potentially rich, joyful, satisfying, and productive relationship possible between two people. Most people, including those who've gone through bitter divorces, want all that marriage can be.

But it's very important to get into a new relationship for the right reasons, and to *be* in a relationship in the right way.

A client came to me to help him navigate his fourth divorce. His pattern had been to get serious with someone new within a few months of getting divorced. Towards the end of the process, I counseled him to remain single for at least a year before venturing into a new relationship. He looked at me aghast: 'I don't like being single! Do you want me to grow old alone?' His complete overreaction to my suggestion told me that he was not going to heed my advice.

A few weeks later when this client came to my office for our final consultation, he was accompanied by a woman (bearing a striking physical resemblance to ex-wife number four) whom he introduced to me as his 'girlfriend'. A few months later they got engaged, and within a year he was back for divorce number five.

Because my client couldn't be at ease with himself when he was alone, he sought a relationship to cover up his unease. The unease then simply reappeared in some other form in the relationship, and he held his partner responsible for it.

Our partners come into our lives to teach us many things. Unfortunately, most people don't know how to learn the lessons, so they repeat the same kinds of patterns in one relationship after another.

Relationships are a great gift, not because they make us happy (they often don't), but because intimate relationships – if we view them as a practice – are the clearest mirror we can find.

The most important ingredient that we put into any relationship is not what we say or do, but *what we are*.

Listen…Really Listen

> We see the world, not as it is, but as we are.
>
> - Anaïs Nin

Most of the time, we don't listen with the intention to understand; we listen with the intention to respond. We're either speaking or preparing to speak. We filter everything through our own paradigms, which we then project on to other people's lives.

'Really listening' means being content to listen to the entire thought of someone, rather than waiting impatiently to respond. This entails learning to listen with a still heart, with a waiting, open soul, and without passion, desire, judgment, or opinions.

If you're willing to be secure enough in yourself to listen – to really listen to what your partner wants or how your partner views a situation, without constantly reacting, objecting, arguing, fighting, resisting, making yourself right and your partner wrong, your partner will feel heard, welcomed, accepted.

Breathe Before You Speak

Our usual harried forms of communication encourage us to criticize our partners' points of view, to overreact, to misinterpret meaning, to impute false motives, and to form opinions – all before our partners have even finished speaking.

'Breathing before you speak' means exactly that. It involves nothing more than pausing – breathing – after your partner has finished speaking.

This practice will immediately result in you having more patience and getting added perspective.

Slowing down your responses and being a better listener will also help you to become a more peaceful person.

Seek First to Understand

> Seek first to understand.
>
> - Stephen Covey

At its essence 'seek first to understand' implies that you become more interested in understanding your partner, and less interested in being understood by your partner.

If you want meaningful, fulfilling communication that nourishes both you and your partner, understanding your partner must come first. That's because when you try to be understood before you understand, communication will break down into a battle of two egos. The merits in both positions then get lost in mutual frustration.

But as each party learns to understand the other, each party's frustration with the other is replaced by compassion.

Partners are Just People Too!

In the real world our partners never come in ideal, perfect form. That 'perfect' person whom we thought we'd gotten together with inevitably turns out to be…well, just a person. Then we get angry.

The problem is not love itself. We run into trouble when we chase after some fairy tale mirage of an utterly fulfilling romance, when we view our beloved as someone who's going to make us happy, who's going to take away all our isolation, loneliness, and suffering. Isn't that how we usually dream of love?

Think of popular professions of 'true love': 'You're my everything!'; 'You complete me!'; 'I can't live without you!' Is the message, *'I love you'*? Not even close. What these really say is, *'my'*, *'me'*, and *'I'*. The message is: *'I need you to make me happy.'*

But when we truly put the focus on someone else, we release ourselves from the boundless anxiety that accompanies the ever-present, nagging, little 'what about me'?

Real love is *never* the cause of suffering.

Real love says: 'I have a passion to be loving.' Attachment says: 'I have a passion to be loved.' Real love says: 'I want you to be happy.' Attachment says: 'I need you to make me happy.'

It is Not About You

We need to start from where we are. We must recognize that we're human beings afflicted with overbearing desires and aversions, and an overpowering sense of self.

Because we cherish ourselves so much, everything our partners do seems to be a reflection on us. Every time you think like this, ask yourself:

> Why is this about me?
> I don't have to take it personally.

If you keep in mind that each of you brought your own baggage to the relationship, it is easier to say, as Shantideva put it:

> Because we are all equal in
> wanting to experience happiness and avoid suffering,
> I should cherish all beings as I do myself.

We all act according to our own levels of delusion. We have to allow our partners to act according to their levels of delusion, and to be more accepting of them. This phrase – *'according to the level of delusion'* – can be an excellent aid to reduce anger and increase forgiveness in a relationship.

I think back to things that my partner did, and I say to myself: 'She was doing the best she could according to her level of delusion.' I think back to things that I did and that I regret, and I can cut myself some slack. I can say to myself: 'I was doing the best I could according to my level of delusion.'

Strive to give up your fierce attachment to the way you want your partner to be. Lighten up! Be accepting and kind.

Do You Want to be Right, or Do You Want to be at Peace?

Arguments arise when you and your partner express your opinions and those opinions differ. Problems creep in when each of you are so identified with the thoughts that make up your opinion, that those thoughts harden into mental positions that are invested with a sense of self, with ego.

When this happens and you then defend your opinions (which are nothing more than thoughts), you feel and act as if you're defending your very self. Unconsciously, you feel and act as if you're fighting for survival.

Your emotions start to reflect this unconscious belief. They become turbulent. You become upset, angry, defensive, or aggressive. You need to win at all costs, lest you be annihilated.

It is no wonder that there's a saying in Zen: *'Don't seek the truth. Just cease cherishing opinions.'* This simply means that you should let go of identification with your mind. Then, who you truly are beyond your mind, emerges.

It's so easy to lose sight of our willing participation in the drama of our lives. If you observe the people around you, you'll notice that they spend almost all of their time defending their points of view. If you relinquish the need to defend your point of view or to convince others that your point of view is the correct one, you'll gain access to enormous reservoirs of energy that had been wasted previously.

When you and your partner have an argument, ask yourself:

> What do I want out of this interaction?
> Do I want to be right, or do I want to be at peace?

We don't like to be corrected. We want others to respect and understand our positions. As we've seen, being listened to, and heard, is one of the greatest desires of the human heart.

Whenever we get angry at our partners when they don't want to accept our positions, we turn 'small stuff' into really 'big stuff' in our minds. We start believing that our positions are more important than our peace. They're not.

I'm not suggesting that there's anything wrong with you being right, only that if you *insist* on being right there's often a price to pay – your inner peace.

If you want to be filled with equanimity, you must choose kindness over being right most of the time. If you want to be at peace, you must understand that being right is almost never more important than allowing yourself to be at peace.

The way to peace is to let go of your position. Let your partner be right. This doesn't mean you're wrong. It only means that you choose peace.

Will This Matter a Year From Now?

Whenever you get worked up over a difference of opinion with your partner, ask yourself this question:

> Will this matter a year from now?

Is this situation really as important as you're making it out to be? Chances are that a year from now you're not going to care (and you might not even remember what the difference of opinion was about). If you're honest with yourself, nine times out of ten you'll realize that it won't even matter ten minutes from now!

This question can give you some much needed perspective.

Choose Your Battles Wisely

'Choose your battles wisely' is a popular phrase when giving parenting advice. But it's equally important to living a contented life. If you choose your battles wisely, you'll not only have fewer battles to fight, but you'll also be far more effective in winning the ones that are truly important.

As you've experienced first-hand, when the tornado that is divorce crashes into your life, life rarely works out exactly as we want it to, and other people rarely behave as we'd like them to. If you fight against this fundamental principle of life, you'll spend your life fighting one battle after the other in endless succession.

To be at peace you must decide consciously which battles are worth fighting, and which are better left alone. If your primary goal in life is not having everything and everyone conform to your expectations, but instead to live a peaceful, relatively stress-free life, you'll find that most battles are not worth it, because they only tear you away from your place of peace.

Be Aware *With* Your Children

When we think of the children in our home as 'our' children or 'my' children, and we start relating to them as our possessions to shape and control so as to satisfy our own desires, we're in deep trouble.

Like it or not, children are, and always will be, their own beings. But they need tremendous love and guidance to come to full humanness.

Our jobs are to protect the children as they develop their own strengths, views, and skills for moving along their own paths that they have to explore with increasing levels of independence.

Just being present yourself, fully aware and available, is one of the greatest gifts you can give your children. Some children who had gone through the trauma of divorce need their parents to be virtually constantly mindful, in addition to the basic nurturing and love and kindness that they need from their parents.

> What can you offer a child? Not things, not a set of social roles. You can offer a child here and nowness; the treasure of consciousness; he treasure of awareness.
>
> - Anonymous

It's a Path

Try not to place the center of your happiness in external things that you can't control – money, possessions, success, or people. Don't hold out for some fairy tale romance. Try to take responsibility for your own happiness, and work towards creating it within.

Remember that mindfulness is a continual path. There will most certainly be lapses and mistakes and setbacks. Skillfulness is required, and developing this skillfulness takes time. Mindfulness is a *practice* that requires courage, persistence, and great patience.

So cut yourself some slack and relax. Tomorrow is a new day.